"*The Adventures of Mighty Mom* just might sav
Diaz provides the inspiration and humor ever
above the challenging circumstances of every

D0829620

Kathy Peel
Contributing editor for *Family Circle* magazine
Author of fifteen books
Has appeared as family management expert for "Oprah"

"With irrepressible good humor, Gwen Diaz escorts her readers
through her own real-life believe-it-or-nots, with a careful look
behind the scenes at how to make mothering work. Every mom will
love the reading, and every mom-to-be needs to have this
delightful prep for hazardous duty ahead."

Jeanne (Mrs. Howard) Hendricks
Well-known author and conference speaker

"Gwendolyn Diaz does a magnificent job of bringing heavenly
principles down to earth. Mothers of all ages will be challenged and
inspired by this book."

Dr. Tony Evans
Senior Pastor, Oak Cliff Bible Fellowship
Well-known author and conference speaker
Host of daily radio program "The Alternative"

"With wit and wisdom, this charming storyteller will touch your
heart, lighten your day, and remind you why motherhood is worth
boarding the roller coaster of childrearing."

Becky Freeman
National speaker and author of many "mom relief" books, including *Worms
in My Tea*, *Real Magnolias*, and *Peanut Butter Kisses & Mud Pie Hugs*.

"Gwen Diaz plays peek-a-boo into her daily mothering moments,
allowing us a glimpse of hope and perspective for our own. Taken
one day or several in a sitting, these devotionals will move you
toward your goal of being a mighty mom!"

Elisa Morgan
President and CEO
MOPS International

"Gwen Diaz has a wonderful way of drawing us into her wild world
of four spirited sons, making us laugh, and then hitting us with
serious truths when our defenses are down. She is a gifted and
animated storyteller, and her carefully-crafted vignettes have a way
of amusing and edifying us at the same time."

Dr. Kenneth Boa
Author of *Simple Prayers*
President of Reflections Ministries

The Adventures of Mighty Mom

By
Gwendolyn Mitchell Diaz

Honor Books
Tulsa, Oklahoma

The Adventures of Mighty Mom:
Here She Comes to Save the Day If Only She Can Find Her Keys!
ISBN 1-56292-773-6
Copyright © 2000 by Gwendolyn Mitchell Diaz
P. O. Box 6206
Lakeland, Florida 33807

Published by Honor Books
P. O. Box 55388
Tulsa, Oklahoma 74155

To Zach, MattE, Ben, and Jonathan
You fill my days with laughter, life, and love.

FOREWORD

This book is for every mother who chose furniture for its ability to blend with peanut butter and jelly while she inwardly longed for white lace; for every mother who ever tied a towel into a cape and then felt an ache in her heart when her little "Superman" grew up and flew off to college. It is for every mother who badly needs a "verbal massage" and some time out for laughter.

With wit and wisdom, this charming storyteller will touch your heart, lighten your day, and remind you why motherhood is worth boarding the roller coaster of childrearing. Tuck it in the diaper bag, leave it by your bed, or put it near the bathtub (my own favorite reading room) and take it out whenever you need a quick Mommy break. Better yet, take a whole "mother's day out" and treat yourself to a leisurely lunch and this wonderful read. You will be blessed.

Becky Freeman
National speaker and author of many "mom relief"
books, including *Worms in My Tea*, *Real Magnolias* and
Peanut Butter Kisses & Mud Pie Hugs.

ACKNOWLEDGEMENTS

So many friends have enriched and filled my life! I wish I could thank them all! Among them are Jeanne Hendricks, who taught me much about family and faith; Pat Bull, who first demonstrated joy-filled motherhood; Ken Boa, who insisted that I share my experiences with others; Jessica Hart, with whom I am learning to pray; and Ed, my faithful husband, who has put up with me through all these years. Thank you all from the bottom of my heart.

INTRODUCTION

A cheerful look brings joy to the heart.

Proverbs 15:30

I guess I should be honest and break it to you right at the start—"Mighty Mom" doesn't really exist! She just sounds a whole lot better in a title than "Regular Mom." (Would you have bought a book called *The Everyday Rigors of Regular Mom?* The publishers didn't think so!) And even though I know exactly where my car keys are at the moment (locked inside the family van!), I am probably not going to be applauded for saving anyone's day today. That is, unless you count things like taking the kids out for pizza instead of serving meatloaf for the third straight day or finding the TV remote. (It had been folded into a newspaper and stuffed in the magazine rack three days ago.)

But in the process of raising four sons, I have learned some things. Early on I discovered that humor helps—a lot! It heals. It relaxes. It changes outcomes completely. If the events of a particular moment don't seem to deserve even the slightest smile, I have found that it is often possible to pick that moment up from its pedestal, turn it around in my hands, and take a look at it from another angle. Almost always there is a glimmer of humor to be found from a different perspective. If not outright laughter, there is often a quiet peace that comes from capturing a tiny glimpse of the situation from God's point of view.

I am blown away when I ponder what an awesome blessing it is to be chosen by God to raise four of His precious children. I am overwhelmed by the responsibility attached to such a privilege. I am humbled by my complete inability to accomplish it without His guidance and help. I have learned that my success or failure as a parent is directly proportionate to my trust in God. I have learned the vital importance and imperative of prayer.

My stories are all part of motherhood—and part of me. I suspect that if you're a mother, you could have written many of them yourself. Perhaps my versions will help you catch glimpses of everyday life from fresh, new angles. I hope they will encourage you and make you smile.

Gwen Diaz

TABLE OF CONTENTS

White Can Wait

Sons are a heritage from the LORD,
children a reward from him.

Psalm 127:3

I'll never quite understand why, but God ordained me to be the mother of four extremely noisy, perpetually active sons. In addition, He blessed me with a male dog; two stray cats (both male); a pair of hamsters which have never produced any offspring (so I can only guess) . . . and then, of course, there's my husband—the one who started it all!

With all these "Y" chromosomes wandering around the house, I find myself missing out on many of the daintier, frillier things in life. I find it hard to justify owning fine china, fancy curtains, and lace doilies while there are five

mud-cleated, soda-splattering, sweaty-smelling males (plus their friends *and* animals) lounging from one end of my house to the other.

I have been dragged to every sporting event and war movie in history. I've watched countless males get gory and "grody." I have yet to find myself seated at a ballet with any of my four sons beside me watching pink swirls of grace and grandeur. (I gave up trying to get my husband to accompany me years ago when I realized that his idea of a cultural event was a professional wrestling match at the Civic Center.)

I miss ceramic rabbits with bows sitting on my windowsills; padded, lace-covered picture albums decorating my coffee table; or flowery placemats accenting, say, a fluffy quiche. And it is with great wistfulness that I recall having once had a wonderful relationship with the color white. . . .

White—as in magnolia blossoms picked early in the morning and set in a china bowl on the breakfast table.

White—as in crisp, cool cotton sheets and spotless lace tablecloths.

White—as in clean, freshly painted, unmarked family room walls.

White—as in the wedding gown, so pure and simple, that got me into all this!

One day, as I was hunting through the summer sales racks, I spied a pair of white shorts. They were sharp. Cool. Clean. Crisp. And just the right size—I *had* to have them!

That evening I bravely donned my new, white shorts and set out for the baseball field. The world took on a new feeling, and I took on a completely new air as I strutted into the ballpark. I felt chic. Proper. Special!

I realized I would have to make some adjustments to keep my fresh, white act together. And I was ready. I firmly kept Ben at arm's length while he ate his purple slushy. Jonathan was not allowed to sit anywhere close to me after diving under the bleachers for a foul ball. Zach and Matthew had to hold their own baseball gear, for once, while they balanced their sodas and pizza after the game. And I refrained from ketchup on my hot dog—just in case.

White is worth it, I thought smugly to myself as I got up to leave . . . only to find myself—and my new white shorts— attached to the metal bleachers by a huge glob of gooey pink bubble gum!

I have now resigned myself to the fact that white and motherhood are incompatible. I guess white will have to wait!

My prayer for today:

Lord, thank You for my children. You must love me very much to trust me with their care. They are truly a heritage—the legacy I will leave behind to do Your work here on earth. Help me be faithful in teaching them Your ways. Give me joy as I patiently toil and persevere in the process. Help me not to allow trivial things—like white—to get in the way. Don't ever let me lose sight of how precious these little ones are to You. As I tuck them into bed tonight, may I treasure them as the reward You intended them to be. Give me a *grateful* heart, dear God.

Amen.

Learning to Land

---

*He lifted me out of the slimy pit, out of the mud
and mire; he set my feet on a rock and gave me a
firm place to stand.*

Psalm 40:2

He was tiny—maybe four years old—when he came to
me and asked for a Superman cape. With very little money
available for the purchase of such frivolities, I fashioned one
from an old blanket and fastened it around my son's
shoulders.

He was thrilled! Off he zoomed, running around and
around the house, jumping off beds, chairs, couches—
anything high enough to be challenging and sturdy enough
to hold his two little feet. Always his cape flowed behind

him, flapping in the wake of his breakneck pace. It was when
he decided to leap from the dining table onto the kitchen
countertop, across the sink, and up onto the refrigerator that
I figured it was time for him to head outdoors.

As I watched him carefully from the window, he ran at
top speed and flung himself into the air across an
embankment which separated our house from
our neighbors'. Over and over he ran his
fastest, leaped with his arms outstretched, and kicked his feet
out behind him. Over and over he landed smack on his belly
and took a huge bite out of our neighbor's sod. Over and over
he dusted himself off, rearranged his cape, and tried again,
fully expecting to take flight. I cringed every time he landed,
but he didn't seem to be in great danger of breaking any
bones or dislodging teeth. I figured that before long he would
tire of the futile attempts and come back inside with a little
less energy to spare.

I became distracted with the busyness of caring for the
other children. When I next glanced out the window, my
attention was drawn to a bright, blue blob at the very tip-top
of the highest orange tree in our side yard. It was Matthew,
poised and ready for a leap of true Superman proportions.

I flung open the window and yelled, "MattE, NO! Don't jump. Wait for Mommy!" I ran outside and used every adult psychological technique I could think of to coax him down from his precarious perch. I even resorted to bribery and the promise of milk and cookies.

Once he was on solid ground, the cape was removed and promptly hidden. We sat down for our promised snack and a discussion of the danger of climbing trees—including the consequences that would follow if he ever tried such a thing again.

"You shouldn't worry about me, Mommy," Matthew insisted as he dunked a cookie in his plastic cup, splashing milk all over the table. "I've learned to land real good when my cape doesn't work. This one you gave me doesn't have a real lot of power, you know."

It's probably something Superman never had to consider, but learning to land "real good" when your cape doesn't work is an important part of life for us humans. Now, some fourteen years later, Matthew is about to take the biggest leap of his life as he leaves home and heads to college. We've created a cape for him over the years, one designed from

many lessons and lots of love. And we've invested this one with special power, the power of prayer.

There are times, because he is human, that Matt's cape won't work. Hopefully we've provided enough opportunities for him over the years to learn to land "real good" on his own. That way, when it does fail him, he can dust himself off with God's grace and love, rearrange his cape, and try again.

My prayer for today:

Thank You, Lord, for the many opportunities You give me to teach my children about Your love and power. I realize that sometimes they are going to "leap" without first looking to You for wisdom and guidance. Thank You for Your outstretched hand that longs to lovingly lift my children up and brush them off when they fall. Help them grasp that hand and not let go. Give me a *trusting* heart, dear God.

Amen.

A Mammoth Memory

These commandments that I give you today are to be upon your hearts. Impress them on your children. Talk about them when you sit at home and when you walk along the road, when you lie down and when you get up.

Deuteronomy 6:6-7

Mrs. Uncapher's third grade class was given an assignment. They were to make a dinosaur replica to go along with a written report, and Jonathan was assigned the Tyrannosaurus Rex, "King of the Tyrant Lizards!"

"Oh boy!" I exclaimed with more sarcasm than enthusiasm. "How are you going to do that? I guess you could make a shadow box, or maybe a clay model. How about a special drawing with salt and yarn glued on top to give it some neat texture?"

"Nope!"

Jonathan immediately informed me that none of the above would do. He wanted to make a papier-mâché dinosaur, just like the one he had seen at the museum, a GREAT BIG dinosaur that would stand up all by itself and look real!

Through the years, our family has completed a great many art projects, and we have a huge closet devoted to craft supplies. However, none of us had ever worked with papier-mâché. I tried to relay this lack of expertise and the problems it might engender to my son, but he was insistent.

"Don't do it!" one of my friends advised me. "It's just not worth the time or effort. So what if he gets a C. Go buy him some play dough. No dinosaur is worth more than ten minutes of your time!"

TIME—that was the *real* issue here. Did I want to invest the time to help my son make a papier-mâché dinosaur when he could get by with something much less time-consuming?

As I looked at the youngest of my four sons in his hand-me-down shirt, broken-off shoelaces, and his brother's favorite baseball cap, I decided that he needed not only my time, but also the attention that went with it. We scrounged through three craft stores before we found instructions on

how to work with papier-mâché. Hours later, after dipping thousands of strips of newspaper into gallons of watery glue and spreading them across an over-sized balloon, our project began to take shape—a round shape—unlike any dinosaur I had ever seen! But it was a start.

Paper towel tubes and hanger wires covered with masking tape became legs and tiny arms. A huge, long tail was added to the spherical body. We fashioned an egg-shaped head on top, and voilá, about five hours into the project we had a . . . well, dinosaur.

Actually, it didn't resemble a dinosaur at all. So we quickly experimented on how to make paper pulp, and by globbing it in various places our project took on a more "dinosaurial" form. That took about two more days.

Altogether our dinosaur project encompassed three days of our lives. In the end, Jonathan was happy. He loved his dinosaur. And I loved the special time we spent together. We talked and laughed. I learned all kinds of third-grade jokes and secrets and a whole lot about my eight-year-old son. He learned a lot about the "olden days" (back when I was growing up). Best of all, we talked about wonderful biblical truths, like God created everything—things as little as ants and as big as dinosaurs—and God knows EVERYTHING you do, EVERYWHERE you are—even when you're hiding under the covers!

Based on my experience, whoever tried to sell us working moms on the idea that when it comes to raising kids the "quality" of time spent is more important than the "quantity" of time had it all wrong. I am more convinced than ever that true quality times can only grow out of quantities of time . . . time spent just being together.

Jonathan and I didn't just make a dinosaur that week. We made a mammoth memory!

My prayer for today:

Lord, just as the moments of my day tick by, so do the opportunities to teach my children about You. Please help me not to foolishly waste the moments You have assigned to me. Give me the desire to seize every opportunity and turn it into a growing adventure in my children's lives. Help me constantly and consistently live out my relationship with You in their presence so everyday tasks turn into joyful, learning experiences. Give me a *teaching* heart, dear God.

Amen.

Everyone Else's Mom

---

*A wife of noble character who can find? Her
children arise and call her blessed; her husband also,
and he praises her: Many women do noble things,
but you surpass them all. Charm is deceptive, and
beauty is fleeting; but a woman who fears
the LORD is to be praised.*

Proverbs 31:10,28-30

There is someone I'm dying to meet. You've probably
heard about her. She's the hero of our younger generation.
They mention her just about every day using nothing but
praise and adulation. It is always with intense feeling and
great admiration that they speak of her.

No, I'm not referring to the latest movie star or the hottest new super model. I'm talking about that someone they refer to as "Everyone Else's Mom." From what I can tell, she must be quite a gal.

You see, Everyone Else's Mom lets her kids stay up past 11:00 P.M. on weeknights and as late as they want on weekends. She agrees with them that sleep is just a waste of life. (I guess her kids never get grouchy.)

Everyone Else's Mom doesn't care if her kids comb their hair or wear belts to hold up their pants when they leave for school. She allows plenty of room in their lives for freedom of expression. Everyone Else's Mom lets her kids Roller Blade to the Circle K for snacks after school—even if there's no sidewalk and all the crossing guards have gone home.

Everyone Else's Mom buys all the "in" clothes and lets her kids wear them whenever they want to. If they get stained with spaghetti sauce or ripped in the back yard, she is happy to replace them. She gives her kids gum on the way to school if they have forgotten to brush their teeth, then reminds them to swallow it before they walk into class.

She finds time to make all the beds by herself, pick up the dirty clothes, take out the garbage, and feed the animals. She is happy to do all these chores so that her kids can relax and watch TV after a long day at school. She thinks it's important for her kids to talk on the phone to their friends for hours, even if they have just spent the whole day together. I'm sure she has already installed a separate phone line for her children, so they will have ample opportunity to develop adequate social and communication skills.

Eveyone Else's Mom never cooks vegetables, always doles out change for soda machines, and even enjoys a little MTV. I've tried for several years to meet this famous lady, but she's awfully hard to pin down. When I ask my children where she lives, they tell me she's at Michael's house, or maybe Jason's, or David's for sure. But if I get around to calling their homes, I am informed that no such lady exists at that address. She quickly disappears, only to reappear at another friend's house—one I don't know quite so well.

I figure that Everyone Else's Mom must flit from house to house lending a "hip" hand or piece of advice. What a woman! I wish she'd show up at my house once in a while

just to help with the laundry! Until she does, I guess my kids will just have to fold their own clothes.

My prayer for today:

Lord, so often I judge myself by what others are saying or doing rather than looking to You. And sometimes I get caught up in being a friend to my children rather than the parent You assigned me to be. I forget so easily that my primary responsibility is to direct them in paths that will honor You. Give me the strength and the wisdom to both love and lead my children. (And once in a while, would You please let them tell me they like me!) Give me a *wise* heart, dear God, one that finds its direction in You.

Amen.

The Latest Doesn't Last

Heaven and earth will pass away,
but my words will never pass away.

Matthew 24:35

The four of them were dressed in bright, flowery jams (the latest in casual attire) and high-top tennis shoes. Their hair, carefully slicked back for the picture, was a lot longer in the back than in the front. Their white T-shirts had a surfing logo on the pockets, and they were sporting sunglasses, each with a different colored frame. The four Diaz brothers staring at me from the picture album were definitely "cooler than cool" that day a dozen or so years ago.

Not too many months later, the jams gave way to workout shorts. Then the workout shorts were stuffed in the

back of the closet in lieu of jeans shorts. The jeans shorts were traded for khakis. Regular khaki shorts soon found themselves in the Goodwill pile in favor of khakis with pockets, which I think are still "in" (at least that's as far as fashion foibles go in the family photo album).

Hairstyles have changed too. (Thank goodness—I never could stand the "'rat tail"!) Shoes have undergone a major, star-induced transformation (in price as well as style). And T-shirts now have strategically placed stripes instead of pictures and photos. (Don't even think about buying one with a pocket.)

An hour spent perusing the Diaz family albums is always good for a lot of laughs. It is also a valuable way to point out the constant flux and fickleness of the fads that our society offers and that we so readily incorporate into our lives.

Remember baseball trading cards and pogs? Now all that the neighborhood kids talk about is Pokémon cards. Yep, the "latest" things don't usually last.

As a matter of fact, we still have an 8-track tape player stashed away in our family room closet. I refuse to get rid of it in case one day it becomes a valuable antique. (Seems every

time I clean out the closets or have a garage sale, I find I've practically given away the keys to a life of ease.) At one time, that 8-track was the hottest item on the shelves of the big new department stores that sprang up all across our nation.

However, 8-tracks were quickly discarded in favor of boom boxes and CD players. Hibachis are considered obsolete compared to countertop grills. And typewriters—they've metamorphosed all the way into computers!

As a matter of fact, there are really only two items I can think of that have consistently been around all of my life. One of them is the safety pin. Think about it. Even paper clips are constantly undergoing changes in style and material. But all we do with the safety pin is find new uses for it.

Walter Hunt of New York first patented safety pins in 1849. Do you ever wonder why such a simple little invention is still around after 150 years, while much more intricate inventions like 8-track players became obsolete in less than five years? It's because people still buy them. Why do people still buy them? Because nobody has ever come up with anything better. Safety pins continue to have current validity in our lives.

Oh, the other item that has been around all my life is—the Bible. I think that may have something to do with current validity, too.

My prayer for today:

Lord, thank You for the reliability of Your message to us in the Bible. Even though times and trends and technologies have changed drastically over the years, Your Word remains current and reliable. Help me not to question its validity for my life. Let it be a source of stability for my family. Give me an *unwavering* heart, dear God, one that finds its strength in the dependability of Your Word.

Amen.

A Table with a Tale

Ask and you will receive, and your joy will be complete.

John 16:24

An old wooden schoolhouse with a huge bell was nestled comfortably in an oak grove just outside Atlanta, Georgia. The exterior remained much the same as it had over the past century. Inside, however, attempts had been made to keep up with the times. New desks and chalkboards replaced most of the original ones. The potbellied stove had been supplanted by a new electric heater. Venetian blinds covered the long windows. A battery-operated clock hung on the back wall.

Yet there still remained a long, sturdy, old-fashioned table in the center of the room. It appeared to be one of the few

original furnishings to survive the many years of elementary enthusiasm and education in that small Georgia town. The solid oak table easily accommodated at least six children at a time, plus their books and papers and pencils and paste. (Do you remember the thick, white kind you used to glop on the back of your papers with a bristly brush? As I recall, it didn't hold projects together very well, but it did taste pretty good!)

The wooden table certainly had received its share of nicks and scratches, doodles and dents. It was probably eager for a restful retirement when it heard the rumors that the school officials had decided to tear the old schoolhouse down. I can imagine it thinking, *Maybe now I can sit quietly in the back of a classroom in a shiny new school and support a row of dictionaries—plus an aquarium with three or four fish. Or maybe I'll be invited into the faculty lounge to hold a pot of coffee and some day-old donuts.*

But noooo!

Someone had to come along and recognize it as the perfect kitchen table for the continually expanding Diaz family—which was desperately in need of more eating space!

You see, a gentleman, who had been invited to a cozy dinner around their tiny table, had heard the family make such a request to God as they bowed their heads to thank Him for their food.

A few days later, he drove past a yard sale at the old school and spied the table on the front lawn. Immediately he recognized it as the answer to the family's prayer. It was loaded onto the back of his pickup truck and dropped off at the noisy house . . . and the poor, old oak table found itself sentenced to many more years of active duty. It complied very graciously, fulfilling a vital role.

Over the years, that kitchen table has become a part of our family. It has been scrubbed and sanded, polished and varnished, and painted several times to match the decor of our various houses.

If you look closely, you can still see the first capital "D" ever scripted by Zach. There are several dents from Matthew's toy hammer, a permanent mark from a pen that missed Ben's paper, and scratches from a spinning top that Jonathan couldn't quite control.

This table has been through a lot. It has held science projects and sewing machines. It has served everything from Cheerios to chicken à la king. It has been draped as a fort and claimed as a castle. It has heard us laugh and cry, pray and sing. It's not the fanciest table that ever held a plate, but it's unique, adaptable, sturdy, and, thanks to a friend and answered prayer, it's ours!

My prayer for today:

I admit, Lord, that it is often only when things get too difficult for me to handle on my own that I turn to You. I forget that You are interested in the small details of my life as well. Help me love You enough to seek Your wisdom and assistance in all aspects of my life—including mundane things like acquiring a kitchen table. Thank You for all the little things You have supplied for me without me even noticing Your hand in them. Give me a *humble* heart, dear God, one that turns to You in every area of my life.

Amen.

A Thump in the Right Place

Listen, my son, to your father's instruction and do not forsake your mother's teaching. They will be a garland to grace your head and a chain to adorn your neck.

Proverbs 1:8-9

I was more than eight months pregnant with my first child. Every inch of my bulging belly ached—inside and out. But I had decided to attempt just one more outing to the mall to pick up one more item for the baby's layette.

All of a sudden I felt something thumping my stomach. It wasn't the usual restless bump or kick from the baby trying to

rearrange my rib cage. It was a different kind of thumping. It actually felt like it was coming from the outside.

Sure enough, it was! It turned out to be the gnarled finger of a little, old lady jabbing me right in the abdomen. I moved back quickly. How rude of her! How dare she touch me. This was *my* private space! It wasn't my fault that I was taking up a little more than usual.

"Young lady," she said, not the least bit put off by my angry scowl. "May I just give you one piece of advice about that wee one inside you?"

She didn't wait even a second for my response, but continued right on in her thin crackly voice. "As you raise this child," (she jabbed again just to be sure I knew which child she was referring to) "you need to remember one thing. Every time you give this child a 'no,' be sure you give him a 'yes' to take its place." She nodded emphatically, then turned and limped away.

That was it. That's all she said before she hobbled down the concourse and disappeared into the bookstore.

For twenty-two years, I have been raising children, and for twenty-two years I have never forgotten those insightful

words. When one of the children was two years old and was found playing with a glass bowl he'd removed from the dishwasher, I remembered that jab in the stomach, and he was given a plastic bowl to play with instead.

When an older sibling tried to swipe a baby brother's rattle, I remembered that crooked finger, and he was taught to make his own "big-boy" rattle using an empty milk jug filled with pennies.

When our eight-year-old was invited to go on a last-minute camping trip with some classmates whose parents we had never met, he wound up having a blast camping out in our own back yard—thanks to the advice of that matron at the mall.

Huge games of Capture the Flag at night were found to be almost as much fun as expensive trips to Disney—compliments of that little lady.

Even now, when a teenager wants to attend a party that might not be well chaperoned, we find ourselves filling the vacuum with an impromptu party at our house . . . yes, based on the advice of a woman whose name I'll never know.

Over the years, instead of just telling our sons that something was wrong, we found ourselves teaching them what would have been right. We learned that raising kids is like growing a garden. You can pull all the weeds you want, but that garden remains nothing more than a bunch of dirt until you plant some vegetables or add a few flowers.

So if you're pregnant, watch out when you go to the mall. You never know when a little, old lady just might walk up to you and jab her gnarled index finger into your stomach. If one does, be sure to heed her advice.

My prayer for today:

Thank You, Lord, for people who care enough to stop and share their life-learned wisdom with those of us who haven't yet traveled as far. Help me to always be open to the advice and admonition of others. And give me godly insight as I direct the children You have lent me down the paths You have chosen. Let my teaching and instruction have beautiful results in their lives—like garlands that will grace their heads. Teach me to look for a "positive" when I must deal with a "negative" so that their hearts will not become hard. Give me an *insightful* heart, dear God.

Amen.

Angels Don't Always Have Wings

May your father and mother be glad;
may she who gave you birth rejoice!

Proverbs 23:25

She was having a hard time buying me gifts. She never knew quite what to get me, so about five years ago, my sister-in-law decided that I needed to start an angel collection. She wrapped my first one and presented it to me that Christmas. It was a beautiful porcelain angel with long delicate wings. Ever since, she has continued to build me one of the most delightful, eclectic collections of angels one can imagine.

However, there was one thing my sister-in-law failed to take into consideration when she selected angels as the object

of my accumulation—the fact that she has four, very active, often rowdy nephews who happen to live in my house!

That, and the fact that most angels are either fragile or frilly, has led to some very interesting moments. Teetering angels have barely been caught as they tipped from the top of the bookshelf. Ruffled, rag doll angels have found baseballs and golf tees sitting in their laps. Wicker angels have nearly been scrunched by low-flying footballs. Shiny, painted angels have been targets for suction-cup darts.

Miraculously, every angel has managed to survive each episode . . . until this morning, that is, which explains why I am typing this with my left hand while the thumb and index finger of my right hand remain interminably stuck together.

Following a wrestling match (which included all four of my sons and their father!), I found my tiniest angel cowering behind the television set, unable to fly back to its home. One of its miniature ceramic wings had been clipped completely off when a flailing limb had sent it flying.

Quite upset, I picked up the itsy pieces and stomped into the kitchen. I hunted in every messy drawer 'til I found the glue that guarantees it can put everything from Humpty Dumpty to china teapots back together again. The

accompanying brochure mentions its special powers to bond paper, rubber, ceramics, leather, and wood.

It forgets to mention one thing: skin!

After two minutes of holding the pieces firmly in place, the only objects stuck together were my fingers! The angel was as wingless as it had been when it first struck the floor.

I approached my sons and tried to plead my case for a kinder, gentler household, but they were much too amused by my lack of gluing prowess to pay much attention.

"Look. Mom glued herself together!"

"I always knew you were stuck on yourself, Mom."

"Mom's just trying to get out of doing the dishes."

"Hey, Mom. What's the difference between an angel with one wing and an angel with two?" one of them quipped.

When I failed to respond, he said, "Not much. It's just a difference of a pinion. Ha, ha, ha. Get it? A *pinion*! That's a big word for a "wing" in case you didn't know, Mom!"

I wasn't amused.

"Come on, Mom, smile. It's just a little ceramic angel. It's not like one of us got hurt or something."

He left the room and came back a few minutes later holding a perfectly glued, deceptively unflawed little angel. And all of his fingers were functioning quite normally.

He handed me the angel and reached over to kiss me on the cheek.

"Did you get it yet? A *pinion* instead of *opinion?*" he asked sheepishly, trying to make me smile.

He succeeded, and I realize . . . I have lots of angels. Some of them are just more rambunctious than others.

My prayer for today:

I realize, Lord, that these gifts You have given me, my children, won't always be perfect. (I guess You could make the same statement about me.) Help me see their lives through Your eyes. Help their characters to be of more value to me than their performance; their heart attitudes more important than the circumstances; their temperaments more important than my trinkets. Don't let me ever get so caught up in my own affairs that I cannot rejoice in the lives of these precious children You have entrusted to my care. Give me a *rejoicing* heart today, dear God.

Amen.

Clothes Don't Make the Woman

*Your beauty should not come from outward
adornment, such as braided hair and the wearing of
gold jewelry and fine clothes. Instead, it should be
that of your inner self, the unfading beauty of a
gentle and quiet spirit, which is of
great worth in God's sight.*

1 Peter 3:3-4

I was out shopping the other day . . . all by myself! That's
right. Not a single child of mine was anywhere in sight, which
meant that no one was dragging me into the electronics
department to check out the latest in computer software. No

one was begging for a new pair of shoes that could make them jump higher or run faster or look cooler than any other kid at school. No one felt the sudden urge to use the restroom or grab a free sample of frozen yogurt. And no one was "dissing" the poor guy dressed like a Chick-Fil-A chicken.

There was only me—all by myself!

As the freedom of the situation dawned on me, a sudden transformation took place within my being. I was no longer a mom at the mall, trying to corral a bunch of energetic sons and do a little shopping at the same time. For a few brief moments, I became someone whose feelings I hardly recognized, someone I had not been in touch with for more than a decade. I became a woman with needs and wants of her own.

I'm not exactly sure who this woman really was or where she came from, but she was obviously a few years younger than I. She thought of herself as somewhat shapely, and she was definitely more daring than most mothers are allowed to be.

It felt good to be her. It felt so good, in fact, that I succumbed to some deep inner urge and made a supreme shopping error. I bought an outfit just for her!

Of course, it was really me who walked into the tiny, trendy "shoppe" sporting gray-skinned, alien-looking mannequins without any eyes. And I was actually the one who tried on the neon stretch tights with the oversized T-shirt. But when I peered into the three-way mirror, somehow a more sophisticated, perhaps even alluring, lady stared back at me. She posed as a model would in front of a row of cameras. She preened as a teenager does in line at the movie theater.

She looked very nice—the saleslady even said so! Then the saleslady talked her into purchasing a matching pair of socks and some colorful, dangly earrings and a scarf that would "bring the whole outfit together." She looked "just darling," according to the saleslady. Who was I to argue! All she needed was a huge, shiny clip to sweep her hair up on top of her head.

I walked out of the store swinging a large, plastic bag filled with new, wonderfully "with-it" clothes. Shopping alone sure was fun! I grabbed a sample of rutti-tutti, pineapple-fruity frozen yogurt, winked at the Chick-Fil-A chicken, and headed home.

I put the outfit on as soon as I arrived—taking extra time
to sweep my hair up in the funky, new barrette—and
modeled it for my husband.

"That's really . . . different," he said carefully, trying not
to get himself in too much trouble during the middle of the
football playoffs.

I decided to ignore him. After all, what did he know
about fashion?

"How do you like my new outfit, guys?" I
bounced in on all four of my sons, interrupting a
brawl over a video game. I figured they would
appreciate my new stylishness.

They barely looked up. A flat "Cool," a "Yeah," and a
"Hmm" were some of the overwhelming responses I received.

"Doesn't anyone like how I look?" I badgered them.
"How about my hair? Do you like it like this?"

I should have known better than to push it. My youngest,
taking the full burden of honesty and tact upon himself,
responded. "Well, Mom," the words drifted out of his mouth
thoughtfully and slowly. "That's just how you would want to

wear your hair . . . if you were young enough to wear an outfit like that."

So much for shopping alone. Next time I'll be sure to take all the kids along. They'd never let me shop in a store where the mannequins don't have eyes!

My prayer for today:

Lord, I want to be known not so much for who I am or what I look like or what I own, but for having a gentle, quiet, godly heart. I admit that I sometimes get caught up in the importance of status or appearance, but I truly desire to be more precious in Your sight than in the sight of others. Help me spend more time today (and every day) looking in Your mirror, the Bible, than in my bedroom mirror. Give me a heart that is *beautiful* in Your sight, dear God.

Amen.

Give a Man a Tractor

*When God gives any man wealth and possessions,
and enables him to enjoy them, to accept his lot and
be happy in his work—this is a gift of God. He
seldom reflects on the days of his life, because God
keeps him occupied with gladness of heart.*

Ecclesiastes 5:19-20

It started twenty-some years ago when my husband was a
fledgling camp director at a brand new camp hidden deep in
the piney woods of East Texas. One afternoon he spied a big
John Deere tractor standing idle in an overgrown pasture.
The property had recently been claimed from the
surrounding forest as grazing land for the camp's horses.

Too many tiresome duties; too many tough decisions; too many late-night, problem-solving parleys caused his mind to revolt. In a desperate effort to get away from it all, he hopped aboard the abandoned tractor, cranked it up, and began to mow.

He proceeded to brush-hog the entire ten-acre pasture . . . as well as the newly christened ball field . . . the paths leading to the dining hall . . . the huge grass parking lot . . . and the median strip on the nearby highway. On and on he mowed, well into the starry Texas night.

Thus began a love affair between a mostly-sophisticated, always-on-schedule man and a powerful machine. He couldn't get enough of tractors—big, green, powerful tractors! If he was missing or late for anything, we could almost always find him high atop a tractor somewhere in the wild hinterlands of the camping world. He loved breathing in the fresh air, smelling the newly cut grass, and drowning out the cares of the world nestled in the seat of a big mowing machine.

However, one day, as with all good things, his camp-directing days came to an end. And none of the suburban homes with suburban lawns in various suburban-type

neighborhoods, into which we subsequently moved, ever required the use of a big, green tractor. A little hand-pushed one always sufficed quite nicely. Sadly, my husband's love affair with tractors languished for lack of opportunity.

Until early one spring, that is. As he drove home from work past an overgrown recreational park one day, he realized that February is about the time that baseball fields all over the city need their yearly makeovers. Mowing the grass, tilling the clay, steel-toothing and dragging the infield all require the use of a tractor. And with four sons often playing on four different teams, surely there had to be a field somewhere that would allow him to do a little extra custodial care. Sure enough, he was right!

I now know better than to look for the man in his office on a late Florida afternoon in the spring. On just about any given day that is fit for a baseball game, I know exactly where I can find him. He will be skillfully maneuvering the base paths of a high school or Little League diamond— breathing in the fresh air, smelling the newly cut grass, and drowning out the cares of the world seated high atop a big tractor, with one of his sons on his lap.

If ever there were a thirty-second chapter for the book of Proverbs, it would probably have a verse that goes something like this:

If a man lacks wisdom . . . let him till the earth.

If a man lacks power . . . give him a tractor.

If a man has sons . . . allow them to dig in the dirt together.

My prayer for today:

Thank You, Lord, for the earth You created for us to enjoy . . . and thank You for filling it up with so many wonderful things. As I get caught up in the busyness of everyday life, help me not to forget the awesomeness of Your creation. Help me to enable others (especially my husband) to enjoy Your gifts and have hearts full of the gladness that come from being close to You. As a family, help us to accept the lot You have given us; to be happy with our tasks; and to take the time to find great pleasure in all that You have provided. Give us *glad* hearts, dear God.

Amen.

Protected in the Pen

No discipline seems pleasant at the time. . . . Later on, however, it produces a harvest of righteousness and peace for those who have been trained by it.

Hebrews 12:11

It was the late 1970s. Our only child was barely a year old and had just begun to toddle his way around the house. Already pregnant with child number two, I decided it would be wise to invest in a second-hand playpen.

I planned to use it only during those ultra-weary times— times when I didn't think I could make one more trip down the hall to snag an escaping toddler or one more dive for a toppling lamp—not to mention the hectic times when two

hands couldn't possibly handle the cooking and the cleaning as well as the corralling of an enthusiastic urchin.

I decided that a playpen was a necessary safety device. It took awhile for him to adapt, but soon my child looked forward to the quiet play times with his special "playpen toys."

Then one evening we had some friends over for dinner. I plopped my one-year-old in the pen while I set the table, stirred the gravy, and filled the glasses with ice.

"You use a playpen?" It wasn't really a question as it projected itself from my friend's mouth. It was more of a shocked exclamation that escaped when she spied my baby happily confined next to the kitchen table.

She continued. "Why would you ever do that to your child? It's so restrictive—so constraining." She was struggling to find "nice" negative words. "I want my children to grow up free and creative," she pontificated. "I'm never going to imprison them in playpens!" She had quickly run out of constructive critiques, but that in no way hampered her.

She leaned over to goo-goo with my poor, incarcerated child while I contemplated whether to pour the ice water in her glass or on her head.

I thought about all the times she had shown up at my doorstep with her yippy, spoiled poodle named Muffi. Every time they arrived, he was on a leash. I had always figured it was because she loved him and wanted to protect him. *Maybe not*, I thought sarcastically. *Maybe it's really because she wants to restrict him and show her dominance.*

I contemplated bringing up the Muffi situation but decided it wasn't exactly the best time for controversy. Silently I poured the water—into her glass—and watched as she set my child *free*. He immediately headed for the fireplace.

Unfortunately my friend's attitude demonstrated the prevailing feeling of the late 1970s. In an effort to antidote the strict upbringing many of us experienced as children, we (as newly assigned parents), overreacted, rendering playpens almost obsolete.

I say unfortunately because three more children and many years later, I am more convinced than ever of the value of playpens. Boundaries will always be an important part of our lives. We can't live without them. We can't even play without them. (What fun would tennis be without a court?)

The earlier children learn to flourish within healthy, safe boundaries, the easier they will adjust to the real world later on. And if we don't impose their first set of boundaries, someone else will have to do it!

My prayer for today:

Help me, Lord, to accept the boundaries You place in my life—boundaries that You designed as a safeguard rather than a restriction. It is tough to remember sometimes that true love necessitates discipline, because discipline doesn't ever seem pleasant at the time. And help me love my children enough to provide boundaries in their lives that won't let them stray into danger and away from You. Please give me a *disciplined* heart, dear God, one that seeks the best for my children.

Amen.

Help, My Kid Is Normal!

My son, if your heart is wise, then my heart will be glad; my inmost being will rejoice when your lips speak what is right.

Proverbs 23:15-16

I overheard a mother talking at the grocery store. On and on she went about her high school child: the clubs he belonged to, the sports he participated in, the offices he held. It didn't seem possible that one child could fit so many activities into his teenage life and do all of them so overwhelmingly well. She pointed out to her friend (and any non-friends within earshot) that his hectic schedule was absolutely necessary if he wanted to get into a *really good* college. An abundance of activities was evidently vital for a good college resume.

It started me thinking. What did my high schooler have that would look good on his resume? "Able to do a perfect imitation of Rainman" didn't seem to qualify. I was sure that "can jump a kneeboard across a wake with the best of them" wouldn't cut it either. How could he ever compete with students like this lady's son who had already traveled through France and Spain, played solos at state competitions since he was six years old, and graduated from space camp—the *real* one, not the one at the local science museum!

I started conniving. I decided that in order to enhance his resume, my son ought to at least run for a class office his senior year. I found him all alone in the kitchen that night with a bag of tortilla chips in one hand and a jar of salsa in the other. This was the perfect milieu in which to broach the subject.

"Have you ever considered running for some sort of class office?" I asked to be subtle.

"No!" he replied trying to be blunt.

He tore open a brand new bag of chips. I decided not to gripe about the already opened bag in the pantry in order to focus on the more important issue at hand.

58

"You ought to." I continued. "It would be a really good experience. You'd be good at it."

He just stared at the label on the salsa jar. I pushed a little more. "I didn't mean president or anything like that."

"Why on earth did you buy salsa made in New York City?" he asked incredulously. "Don't you ever watch TV commercials?"

I obviously wasn't getting through.

"How about vice president? You're pretty popular and, besides, no one else is running."

His sideways glance spoke quite clearly, "Mom, you're really starting to bug me." But I felt it was worth at least a little more effort.

"You never know. You might really enjoy it if you just give it a try."

"Uh-uh," he muttered emphatically and shook his head. His mouth was too full of salsa and chips to utter anything more eloquent.

I was losing ground, so I decided to lay all my cards on the table in full view. "Well, you ought to consider it if you

want to go to a really good college. It would look great on your college resume—and you don't have much to put on one right now. Student government holds a lot of prestige."

That did it. He stopped in the middle of dipping a chip and looked me straight in the eye.

"Mom," he said, "the answer is 'No.' I don't do student government. I do sports, and I get good grades. If that's not good enough to get me into a 'really good' college, then I'll just go to a normal one. I happen to think that there are plenty of good colleges out there that would love to have someone like me!" A big glop of salsa landed on his shirt. He rolled his eyes and then licked it off.

He was right! He leads a wonderfully focused, uncluttered life. He works hard at the sports he has selected, gets good report cards, and attends youth functions at our church regularly. He really enjoys being a teenager. Why do I insist on pushing for more, asking him to pretend to be someone he's not?

He stuffed the chips back in their place on the shelf (next to the already opened bag) after he had stuffed me back into mine. Sometimes it's tough raising a teenager who enjoys being normal!

My prayer for today:

Lord, please help me not to connive and push and try to make my children more than You desire them to be. Help me to view their present lives with joy, rather than trying to manipulate their futures. My desire is that they please You with their attitudes more than they please the world with their accomplishments. Help me rejoice in their wisdom and godliness much more than in their status. Give me a *properly focused* heart, dear God, one that understands what is really important in my children's lives.

Amen.

The Big Boo from the Balcony

When I was a child, I talked like I child, I thought
like a child, I reasoned like a child. When I became
a man, I put childish ways behind me.

1 Corinthians 13:11

This story took place several years ago—long enough that
I can relate it to you without total embarrassment (and maybe
even with a giggle). It took place one Sunday morning at
church. Actually, it started the day before at the ball field. . . .

You see, some friends of ours had given us tickets to a
Detroit Tiger's spring training game. It was the first adult
baseball game that our four boys had ever been to, and they
took it in with wide eyes and open ears. They were fascinated

by everything—the batting practice, the foul balls that flew over their heads, the hot dogs in the "squished" buns, the cheering, the booing . . . yes, particularly the booing.

Not only was it their first real baseball game, it was the first time in their lives that our boys had ever been exposed to real-life booing. And the man in the seat behind Matthew was indeed a master boo-er. He booed EVERYTHING from the groundskeepers to the managers; from the umpires to the hot dog vendors. And he did it all with great gusto.

Matthew, who was about five years old at the time, was entranced. For the first few innings, he just sat there staring back at the big booing mouth behind him. About halfway through the fifth inning, however, he decided to get in on the action, and cued by the gentleman (I use the term loosely) behind him, he became a bona fide boo-er. It was all rather funny and cute . . . until the next day.

Our church is very large and very proper. We happened to be celebrating our 100th anniversary. It was a very special service with bell choirs, bagpipes, and red-robed ensembles, so I decided it would be a good idea to take the children into the sanctuary with me instead of depositing them in children's church as usual. My husband was out of town (of

course), so the children and I sneaked quietly into a corner of the balcony.

After many beautiful, but rather lengthy, musical selections, an elder of the church began to introduce everyone who had been a member of the church for fifty years or more. You wouldn't believe how many people fit into that category. The list went on and on.

We had been asked to hold our applause until the end, so when the long list was finally completed, we all stood and clapped very formally, very decently, very properly. All except for one of us, that is. Louder than all the thousands of clapping hands was—you guessed it—the sound of Matthew booing from the balcony. I couldn't believe it. There he stood. His neck muscles were straining. His face was bright red. He was booing with all his heart just like the man at the ball field. I was mortified!

As I said, this happened several years ago. Matthew is now nineteen and has learned to boo a little more appropriately. He is even allowed back in church on rare occasions.

Last week, I actually laughed as a friend and I recalled the event. I didn't turn red or stumble for excuses or blame the man at the stadium. I just plain laughed out loud. It was nice to

realize that time not only matures our children in stature and wisdom—time also has a sense of humor. And, given enough time, even mortification can have its moment of mirth.

My prayer for today:

Lord, I'm sure that when You, as my Father, look at various incidents in my life, You are mortified. How could anyone claiming to be Your child behave so impatiently or insensitively or with such misplaced emotion? Forgive me for all my childlike behavior. Help me to grow not only in my knowledge of You, but also in my behavior and character. Help me, as Your daughter, to make You proud and bring You joy. And in doing so, help me be a mature example to my children. Grant me patience when they act immaturely. Give me a *growing* heart, dear God—one that seeks to please You.

Amen.

How to Cross a Raging River

If the Lord delights in a man's way, he makes his steps firm; though he stumble, he will not fall, for the Lord upholds him with his hand.

Psalm 37:23-24

My years spent growing up as a missionary kid in the heart of Africa were intensely fascinating. I witnessed incredible wildlife, dined on exotic cuisine, and was surrounded by majestic scenery. It was the kind of life that most children only read about in books or watch on public television shows.

I hiked deep into jungles, climbed atop extinct volcanoes, and crossed raging rivers. However, life wasn't all "Shangri La." Everywhere I went, I was surrounded by intense poverty, devastating disease, and constant crises. There were new lessons to be learned each day, and most of them dealt with survival.

I learned to hunt guinea fowl, plant peanuts, and harvest only the edible dates. I adapted to an existence without electricity or running water, yet was able to wash my own clothes and make ice cream sandwiches. I could recognize the whine of a leopard kitten, trap a cobra in its hole, and shelter my face from the Sahara sands. I also discovered how to cross a raging river without being swept off my feet. It was a lesson the natives had learned many centuries before.

As each African tribesman approached a river, he would select a rock (the heavier the better), hoist it onto his shoulder, and cross through the water carrying the boulder as ballast. The extra weight kept his feet firmly on the bottom of the riverbed so he wouldn't be swept away. Once across, he would leave the rock on the bank for the next traveler planning to cross in the opposite direction.

I first carried my own ballast across a small river that separated our home from our garage (six miles away). There were no bridges across the Bunga River, so our car stayed on the far side of the river most of the year. The first few years of my life I was carried across the water on the shoulders of a strong tribesman. But as I grew, so did my responsibilities; and by the time I was six, except during the torrential rainy season, I was responsible for carrying my own weight. It was often difficult, but never once was I swept downstream by the current or hurled against a hidden rock like a rag doll.

I was reminded of this lesson as I overheard a conversation in a doctor's office the other day. Several mothers were talking about their children, discussing the schools they attended, their ball teams, etc. During the conversation it became apparent that there were several teachers or coaches or tough situations that these parents did not want their children to have to experience. They were willing to go to great lengths to keep their youngsters from being placed in a position that would cause them to struggle.

I thought about my own children. I remembered the time one of them got "stuck" with the teacher everyone tried to

avoid; how I tried to remove him from the situation, but found no way out. I recalled how my child struggled under her tutelage, was forced to adjust, and eventually excelled in her classroom. I realized what a blessing it was that he had been exposed to this very difficult experience while he still lived at home—while we were still there to help him learn to adjust and cope and mostly pray! I realized how much wiser and stronger he had become through the struggle and how much closer he had grown in His relationship with God.

It is no wonder so many of our children are swept off their feet when they come to difficult crossings in their lives. It's a natural tendency in parenting to try to protect them from difficulty. We don't want them to struggle when we know we could easily provide a solution. We forget that we can't carry our children all their lives. At some point they need to cross the rivers of life on their own. They need to learn to turn to God for help, rather than their parents. There are so many currents we can't control, which will pull them strongly in wrong directions. The sooner they learn to carry their own "ballast," the better able they will be to keep their feet on the ground.

My prayer for today:

Lord, give me the confidence to trust my children to Your care. Keep me from rushing in to rescue them whenever they stumble. I realize that You have valuable lessons for them to learn. Help me allow them to struggle sometimes, so that they will turn to You. Only when I let go can they grasp Your hand. Give me the wisdom to know when to allow them to carry their own "ballasts." Give me a *confident* heart, dear God—one that knows Your hand will not let my children fall.

Amen.

Life Isn't Exactly a Video Game

This is the day the LORD has made;
let us rejoice and be glad in it.

Psalm 118:24

"Too bad life isn't a video game," our youngest said with a sigh much too deep for his age. "Because if it was, I'd just push the reset button and start this day all over again."

Jonathan was lying prone in the back seat of the station wagon. His right leg was propped up on two pillows. A baggie full of ice kept sliding off the huge knot in the middle of his shin while a puddle of mud and ice water collected on the

71

seat beside him. It was about 5:30 P.M., and we were on our way to the emergency room.

It certainly had been one of those days—one you wish you could just forget completely or at least start over; one you wish you could manipulate with a joystick.

Relatives had been visiting for more than a week. We were starting to run low on food, hot water, and creative things to do with three extra kids in the house. If life had been a video game, we could have "powered up" at the beginning of the day and made it through with energy to spare. But somehow joysticks don't work on kids who get grouchy when they can't take a hot shower. That morning we had made a quick trip to IHOP, spending lots of money (and spilling lots of syrup) in order to provide a breakfast treat and, hopefully, an attitude change.

Around noon our newly acquired puppy from the SPCA had decided it preferred the terrier's grown-up dog food to its own puppy chow. This led to a dogfight which would have made any World War II fighter pilot cringe. If it had taken place within the confines of a video game, we would have merely pushed pause at the first sign of trouble and avoided

the whole incident. But video game controls do nothing when there's real blood and guts being spilled in the back yard. We had to bodily intervene before the battle became too messy.

Then that afternoon, when we took the new puppy to the vet for his first checkup, we were informed that the SPCA had been wrong. The animal we had chosen was not even close to six months old yet, nor did he weigh a full-grown twenty-five pounds. He was actually a whopping thirty-five pounds and less than half his adult size!

We soon realized that the handwritten statement on his certificate of adoption was open to interpretation. "A smart dog; paper trained" must have meant that he could read the daily news, because he certainly didn't know what else to do with the morning paper. If this had been a video game, we could have just started all over, selecting a smaller mutt as our player—one that would fit through our new, expensive doggy door when it was full-grown. But video games don't have to account for children's emotions. Real life does. So, after much discussion and many tears, the huge, untrained, baby mutt was allowed to stay.

73

It was after all this that the incident which caused the severe pain in Jonathan's right shin occurred. He was shagging baseballs for his older brothers when, somehow, his right leg got caught in the chain link fence. As he fell, it twisted, snapping both the bones in his lower leg.

If one of the players in his video baseball game runs into the fence or otherwise flubs up a catch, I know that Jonathan just conveniently pushes "reset" and begins the inning all over. (This annoys his older brothers to no end!) But there was no way for us to go back half an hour and run Jonathan's last play in a different direction, so we were stuck going to the emergency room.

"You know, what's the problem with real life?" Jonathan pondered out loud as he lay in the back seat of the station wagon continuing to contemplate his video game analogy. "Everything counts!"

He was right. There was nothing to do but make the best of the situation—so I promised him a new video game when he got home from the hospital.

My prayer for today:

Lord, I realize that things won't always go the way I want them to—that's for sure! Please give me the understanding that You have a plan for each new day. No matter what situation comes my way, whether good or bad, help me trust in You and rejoice in Your watchful care over me and my family. Give me an *accepting* heart, dear God, one that is willing to find peace in Your plans.

Amen.

Mildewed Moms

Let us not become weary in doing good, for at the
proper time we will reap a harvest
if we do not give up.

Galatians 6:9

A few years ago El Niño hit with a vengeance, wreaking
havoc all across the nation with devastating mud slides in
California, unparalleled winter storms in the northeast, and
rain—lots and lots of drenching, flooding rain where we live
in Florida. We were very fortunate, however. Through all the
heavy storms, we never had to bail out our living room with a
bucket or wade across the street to get to the mailbox or
ferry our kids to the bus stop in a john boat as many of our
friends did.

The biggest problem we had to deal with was the moss and mildew that the weather left behind. We didn't even realize it was growing until one dark day when we had to pick up some fallen tree branches. We noticed that everything in the backyard was covered with slimy, green stuff.

The picnic table on the deck had taken on a strange greenish hue. (Actually it matched the railing on the deck quite nicely.) The trampoline presented a new slick challenge to anyone brave enough to jump. The garage doors were slimy, and parts of the driveway were so slippery that it was considered a dangerous job (worth at least a 25 percent increase in allowance) to take out the garbage. Everything was dank and dingy and slimy and greenish black. There was a blah feeling  pervading the whole backyard. It was downright depressing.

When I noticed that the terra cotta angels on the bird feeder had bright green faces, I decided it was time to start a massive mildew removal project. It's amazing what a little Clorox and water, along with a scrub brush, can do to brighten things up. Add a little sunshine, and it's a bright new world!

While we were scrubbing, one of our sons recollected the time we had spent cleaning the yard together several years

before after a tropical storm had ripped through our neighborhood. We had surprised the children afterward with a fishing trip and picnic at the pond as a special treat for being such great helpers.

Then another remembered the time we had let them climb high into the oak trees to cut down mistletoe. They laughed, recounting how we had tied it with bright red ribbons and sold it to gracious neighbors for fifty cents a bundle. We were off and running down memory lane.

One recalled the time we had summoned them individually to the principal's office at school. Each of them then chimed in and shared the feelings of trepidation they had experienced as they trudged to the office, one at a time. It turned out that we were taking them to a spring training baseball game (during school hours!).

They remembered special notes hidden in their lunch boxes and little surprises tucked under their pillows at night. We were all smiling and laughing as we recalled different memorable events, until one of them sighed wistfully and commented, "It's been a long time since we did neat stuff like that!"

My smile faded quickly. I had to admit he was right. That's when I realized that parenting can quickly become as mildewed as any backyard. It was definitely time to freshen up my parenting—as well as my terra cotta bird feeder.

So the next day I bought Corn Pops at the grocery store, because . . . well, just because none of my kids had ever had Corn Pops for breakfast before! Hey, it wasn't much, but at least it was a start.

My prayer for today:

Lord, You have given me one of the most important tasks in all of creation, that of being a mother. Thank You for trusting me to raise these precious children for You. Help me not to grow weary in carrying out the chores and responsibilities involved. Cause me to get out of bed each morning with renewed joy and excitement. Prompt in me a desire to seek fresh, new ways to brighten and fill our days. Give me an *enthusiastic* heart, dear God . . . one that refuses to grow weary.

Amen.

Pressure to Perform

[Parents], *do not exasperate your children;*
instead, bring them up in the training
and instruction of the Lord.

Ephesians 6:4

He was bored. It was the last week of his summer vacation. His three older brothers were out of town. He had used up every penny of the funds set aside for vacation trips and treats. Now he was stuck at home with nothing to do.

Our son was about to go stark raving mad. He had wandered around the house aimlessly for hours searching for something to occupy his time. Much to his dismay, I decided to put him to work cleaning out closets. That's when he came across the old Yamaha guitar stashed away in the back corner of the family room closet. It was one of the last vestiges of my

husband's hippie days, and it hadn't been played in close to twenty years.

He opened the ragged cardboard case and gently lifted the wooden instrument to his lap. He adjusted the red-flowered strap and slung it over his shoulder. Carefully, one at a time, he fingered each string, adjusting the tension with the rusty knobs until he had brought each one into some sort of musical alignment.

Then he began to strum. Within a few minutes he had mastered several chords, and throughout the next week, whenever he escaped for a spare moment from his closet cleaning chores, he gravitated to that guitar and played until his fingers turned purple and calluses formed.

He found enough loose change in an old piggy bank to buy himself a chord book, and by the time school started, his musical skill on that beat-up, old guitar had advanced rapidly. Over the next two months, whenever his homework was finished and his chores were completed, he sat down with the guitar. Never once did he complain of boredom. The music seemed to relax and inspire him. He was a happy child when he was strumming his guitar.

Two weeks ago, I walked in on him. He was accompanying himself in a perfect '60s rendition of "Brown-eyed Girl," picking each chord like an old pro. Enthusiastically (and naively), I stepped into the situation.

"You have gotten so good at this," I remarked in complete awe of his new ability. "Why don't we get you some lessons?"

I thought he would jump at the opportunity. Instead, he politely but bluntly turned me down.

"No thanks, I don't think I need them. I'm doing just fine by myself," he insisted.

"I'll pay for them." I persisted.

So did he. "Lighten up, Mom. What's the matter? Don't you like the way I play?"

I was shocked by his response. But I started to think about it. I thought about how much fun he used to have playing soccer in the back yard—before we decided he should play on a "real" team. I remembered how competitive it had become; how everyone had pushed him to excel; how he had quit after just a couple of seasons; how exasperating the whole experience had been.

82

I realized that I was about to do the same thing with his guitar playing. I was about to turn his main source of relaxation and creativity—a time of personal reflection and accomplishment—into a project where practice and performance were dictated. The last thing he needed in his life was more pressure.

I followed half of his advice. I lightened up . . . but I didn't leave. I love "Brown-eyed Girl," especially the way he plays it!

My prayer for today:

Lord, I know that excellence is not linked to performance in Your eyes, yet I so easily fall prey to that pressure from society. Help me seek excellence for my children in their spiritual lives more than in their physical lives. Help me understand that they need quiet times just to relax and revive their bodies as well as their souls. Don't let me exasperate them by always pushing them to perform. Give me a *relaxed* heart, dear God, one that allows my children to advance and grow at Your pace rather than my own.

Amen.

Removing the "Trailer Wheelers"

Train a child in the way he should go,
and when he is old he will not turn from it.

Proverbs 22:6

He was rough and tough and three years old and attacked every moment of life at full speed. He could hit a wiffle ball off the tee in the back yard all the way past the picnic table and scurry around the bases while his older brothers chased it across the neighbor's yard! He could jump off a swing at full height and land clear in the middle of the flower beds! He even climbed a workman's ladder onto the roof one day just to check out how the birds were doing.

From the moment he got up in the morning 'til he dropped from exhaustion at night, he wanted to be outdoors exploring, digging, creating, and discovering. There was always dirt on his face, a scratch on each knee, and some sort of "treasure" in his pocket.

One day while I was busy weeding my trampled flower bed, a grubby index finger tapped me on the shoulder, and a husky voice demanded, "Mommy, take my trailer wheelers off."

We had been given a little, red bicycle when our oldest son was four. It came equipped with a set of little, red training wheels. Both of our older sons had learned to ride on it, and now it was Ben's turn. But he was barely three. I thought my husband was pushing it when he had removed the training wheels for the others boys just after they turned four. But following a few practice runs, with Dad running along behind (then dropping exhausted onto the pavement), each of them had taken off into the exhilarating world of bike riding.

Later they graduated to larger vehicles, leaving the little, red bicycle to Ben—who immediately dumped his Hot Wheels for this new and greater challenge. We reinstalled the

training wheels ("trailer wheelers" in Ben talk) and set him free to follow his brothers around the five-acre lot next to our house. Just a few days later, Ben made his request.

I figured there was no way a three-year-old was ready for the challenge of balancing on two wheels down a bumpy driveway. I told him to practice real hard, and maybe when he was four I would take them off. I felt he still needed the protection and security the training wheels provided.

Practice he did! Day after day, he zoomed around on his little, red bike with its red "trailer wheelers"; and day after day, he begged me to remove them. Finally, one day, just to reward his intense efforts, I decided it was worth a try even  though he was only three. And sure enough, when I ran out of breath and let go of the seat, he took off all by himself with the biggest grin you can imagine on his face.

Well, Ben is about to enter his senior year in high school, and we just took off his "trailer wheelers" once again. No. Not the extra set of little, red wheels on his bike. This time it was his curfew. For the next year Ben will be on his own to determine what time he needs to get himself home, and to figure out exactly how much sleep he really needs. We experimented with this on our older boys and found that it works great. By the time they arrived at college, they no longer felt the need to experience the outer limits of their newfound freedoms, as most freshmen do.

Little by little, as our children have matured, we have removed things that previously provided security and protection. Little by little we have set them free to tackle the world on their own—while we're still around to pick them up if they fall! Little by little they have grown into independent young adults.

And it all started with a set of little, red "trailer wheelers."

My prayer for today:

Lord, please give me the wisdom to know when to let go; when to set my children free to grow and learn on their own. Show me creative, intelligent ways to allow them to mature. May they grow into responsible young adults who have developed their own relationship with You; responsible young adults who don't need me there to point out right from wrong when they leave the boundaries of our home. Give me a *releasing* heart, dear God, one that allows my children to mature mentally, emotionally, and spiritually.

Amen.

Scared
"Kindless"

The only thing that counts is faith expressing itself through love.

Galatians 5:6

I noticed him for the first time last summer. He was sitting on a park bench watching some children feed the swans. He was a young man with long, tangled hair—definitely in need of a bath. He wore a thick, brown jacket even though the temperature was close to ninety degrees, and he was clinging to a large, tattered satchel. There was a smile on his face, and he seemed to be enjoying a quiet afternoon by the lake.

Later that week I saw him walking past the police station— still wearing the brown jacket, still clinging to the tattered satchel, and still wearing a bemused expression on his scruffy face. He seemed to be heading somewhere, but he certainly

88

wasn't in any hurry. I've seen him several times since then at several different locations. Always, he has been wearing his jacket and carrying his satchel. Always, he has been smiling, at least with his eyes. And always, he has been alone.

Then last week I saw him at the library. He was absorbed with the contents of the *Wall Street Journal*. At first I wasn't sure it was the same man, but then I noticed the jacket on the back of his chair and the satchel stuffed under the table next to him.

I kept checking on him as I tried to do my research. I wondered who he was and why he was always alone. I wondered where he lived and why he had so much spare time. I wondered if he was hungry.

I concluded that he must be homeless and that the library was probably a pleasant place for him to go for rest and refuge. I figured that he must be pretty smart and not strung out on drugs or hung over from alcohol— otherwise how could he be deciphering the latest business trends? He didn't appear to be a mean person (he had a constantly pleasant expression on his almost boyish face), but he obviously didn't have very many friends or much of a family.

I decided to ask him if he would like to spend Thanksgiving Day at our house the next week. I reasoned that he could probably use a good meal, and he seemed to enjoy being around people. Besides, it would be a good opportunity for my children to learn to share with someone less fortunate.

Then I remembered the story that had appeared on the news a few nights before. It was about a lady in California who felt pity on a homeless man. She had found him huddled on a park bench in a pelting rainstorm. This Good Samaritan drove him to her home, gave him a towel, and sent him to her son's room to rest while she cooked dinner. Meanwhile, her husband flipped on the TV, and there, staring at them from the set of "America's Most Wanted," was their house guest!

I couldn't imagine that "my" homeless man had ever done anything wrong. But, then again, why was he homeless?

I sat there watching him as he picked up *Psychology Today*, and wrestled with the decision I had to make. Reluctantly I decided that with four children, I couldn't take the risk of bringing a stranger into our home.

Once again we would eat our traditional holiday meal with
our traditional holiday friends. *It's sad,* I
thought, *but the violence in our society has*
scared the kindness right out of me. Then I
remembered the Salvation Army and the
soup kitchen, and the many other places
that provide opportunities to serve and love.
Someone could sure use some help, I decided. It turned out to be
our best Thanksgiving ever!

My prayer for today:

Sometimes it's hard to give away love, Lord, in such an
unfriendly world. But I know that it is the ability to find a
way to do so that should set Your children apart from the rest
of humanity. Help me not to give up easily. Show me the
ways You want me to display Your love to others today. And
give me the wisdom to teach my children safe and wonderful
ways to demonstrate Your concern for the well-being of those
around them. Please give me a *kind* heart, dear God, even in
a dark and unfriendly world.

Amen.

Stay within the Lines

But the man who looks intently into the perfect law that gives freedom, and continues to do this, not forgetting what he has heard, but doing it— he will be blessed in what he does.

James 1:25

"Stay within the lines. The lines are our friends," the prune-faced man instructed. I had just flipped on the TV as the teacher in the commercial was addressing a class of well-mannered, well-manicured kindergarten students. However, he was quickly disobeyed and discredited by a snooty, tousle-haired, redhead who deliberately began to scribble all over her coloring paper, completely disregarding the carefully drawn lines.

Suddenly, she morphed into a sassy, young adult and sped off down the highway behind the wheel of her brand new, bright red, sports utility vehicle. And sure enough, it wasn't long before she veered across the well-marked lines of the highway onto the rugged terrain of the untamed, unexplored, unlined countryside. She portrayed the very essence of freedom as she broke away from the lines that once restricted her.

I immediately wanted an off-road vehicle of my own. I, too, wanted to feel the freedom of flying across some remote field with the wind blowing in my hair and my daily routine shattered to smithereens—no boundaries; no time constraints; nothing to stand in my way. It was all so appealing. As a matter of fact, it was a little too appealing.

I didn't have a bright, red sports vehicle, but that wasn't about to stop me. Quickly I scribbled a note: "Out to have fun. Back whenever I get here!" and headed off in my station wagon (otherwise known as The Grocery-getter), with the windows rolled down and the radio turned up. I was free!

I traveled away from town toward the only countryside that I knew, and for about thirty minutes I twisted and turned down long, lonely country roads. I was ecstatic! Not even a slow-moving truck pulling a ditch-digger could bother me that

day. I just scooted past it on the gravelly shoulder of the road. I was definitely intoxicated with my newfound freedom.

Everything was perfect . . . until I heard a funny knocking in my engine and spied a red light on the dash. I glanced at my oil-change sticker and realized that I was about 1,000 miles overdue. It was probably time to head home. I turned around on the side of the road taking a piece of a barbed wire fence with me, and began backtracking.

I knew that all the left turns I had previously taken would now have to be right turns; and that all my right turns would now have to be left ones in order to make it home. But somehow, I missed one of them. And you guessed it, I was lost—very lost! Soon I was lost and angry. My hair was blown into a frazzle from the windows being down. There was dirt in my eyes, and the radio was playing music that was much too loud and far too happy.

Being female, I didn't hesitate to ask for directions at the first sign of humanity, but it was several hours before the car and I limped slowly into the driveway.

That afternoon I realized something about life and lines. Lines can be pretty important. The snappy commercial had forgotten to mention that there is no such thing as total

freedom. For every freedom there is always a corresponding obligation or "line."

You cannot be free to play tennis unless you play within the lines. You cannot freely fly a kite without a string attached. You cannot drive a car without oil or get home without directions or leave the highway without hitting lots of bumps.

I guess life is full of lines and responsibilities . . . and sometimes the lines *are* our friends.

My prayer for today:

Help me, Lord, to comprehend the importance of the lines You have drawn for me—the boundaries You have so carefully delineated in Your Word. Help me not to carelessly disregard or purposely ignore any of them. Help me grasp the wisdom and love which went into the creation of each one. They are Your means of providing me with protection and guidance. Help me demonstrate a willing and joyful obedience so my children, too, will want to follow You. Give me an *obedient* heart, dear God, one that rejoices in the lines You have drawn.

Amen.

The Problem with Prayer

This is the confidence we have in approaching
God: that if we ask anything
according to his will, he hears us.

1 John 5:14

I woke up early one morning just a few days ago. The sky was bright and sunny. My day was booked from dawn 'til dusk with important activities. There were deadlines to meet, chores to do, and children to cart all over the county. I was ready to roll.

"God," I prayed, "please give me the strength to make it through this day, and somehow, in the midst of everything, teach me FLEXIBILITY. In all my planning and scheduling, I

don't want to forget that Your plans are more important than mine."

That was the day it rained—and I don't mean drizzled. The sky suddenly clouded over with rolling, rumbling clouds, and hail came pounding from the heavens. All activities were canceled. Instead of hustling to ball games and band practices, we scurried around trying to cover our cars and protect our animals.

That was the day my son had to be rushed to the emergency room for stitches in his gaping knee.

That was the day the toilet backed up on the second floor, and sewer water seeped through the floorboards and out the light socket in the pantry.

That was the day my husband told me he hated our house, which I had talked him into buying six years before, and he wanted to move.

The next morning I woke up. The weather was miserable. "God," I prayed, "please teach me PATIENCE today. I'm really going to need patience with the kids on a rainy day, patience with my husband who hates our house, and patience with all the overpriced plumbers who don't ever show up when they say they will."

That was the day the plumber got his truck stuck in the mud next to the driveway and spent all day unsticking it and using my phone—while I paid his exorbitant fee and had to use the toilet next door.

That was the day my husband backed his car into the neighbor's mailbox while trying to avoid hitting the plumber's truck—and swore it was because our driveway was built incorrectly (One more reason to hate our house!).

That was the day my son forgot his "most important homework assignment of the year!" and needed it immediately. About the time I got it to the school he realized that he'd also forgotten the belt for his baseball uniform, which was "much, much more important" than the silly English assignment I had just spent half an hour rushing to his school! That entire day I didn't accomplish one single thing on my two-day-old to-do list. I was ticked.

After a much-needed night's sleep, I awoke. I didn't even notice the weather. I just prayed and asked God to teach me HUMILITY. "God, please don't let me get all caught up in my

own needs and lists and agendas today. Help me see life from Your point of view."

That was the day I had decided to do something about the gray hairs that were sprouting from the top of my head, but my hair wound up a "peculiar purple" instead of a "brilliant brown."

That was the day the plumber called me and told me that my pantry was such a mess that he couldn't get to the light socket to fix it while I was out fooling with my hair. He'd have to come back another day . . . and, by the way, he was sorry about the truckload of mud he had tracked across my already dirty kitchen floor!

That was the day my children informed me that they didn't like most of my cooking. And from all his little innuendoes, I could tell that my husband thought I had bad taste in hair color, as well as houses.

* * *

"God, as I wake up this morning I have just one request. Please, please don't teach me ANYTHING today. I'd rather just be stupid—if that's okay with You!"

My prayer for today:

What a privilege it is to be able to come into Your presence, Lord, and know that You will hear me. You are the awesome, sovereign God of the universe, yet You allow me to make requests of You! Help me not to take such an awesome opportunity lightly. Help me come before You with praise and humility. There is so much You want to teach me each day. Give me the wisdom to recognize Your hand at work in my life. Help me grasp what areas You are seeking to change today; then give me the desire to allow You to make the necessary changes. Give me a *pliable* heart, dear God.

Amen.

Victim or Volunteer?

*Whatever you do, work at it with all your heart, as
working for the Lord, not for men, since you know
that you will receive an inheritance from the Lord as
a reward. It is the Lord Christ you are serving.*

Colossians 3:23-24

In a moment of naive enthusiasm, I volunteered. It would
only be for a couple of hours a week, I figured. And the
season would only last through the fall. Two of my children
were already on the squad, and the coach really needed help.
So it was perfectly logical that I should volunteer to be the
team mom for the Vikings soccer team. Right? How hard
could it be anyway?

I stayed late after the first practice to be apprised of my duties.

The coach began rather nonchalantly. "Well, basically all you have to do is provide drinks every Saturday for our half-time break. Just be sure they are full of electrolytes and won't make the kids puke when they start running down the field during the second half of the game."

"Great! I can handle that," I said as I shook his hand, smiled, and turned to go.

"Some team moms like to provide something special after the games, too—like a soda or candy bar," he quickly added.

 "Okay. I'll take care of that," I responded. I didn't feel the need to shake his hand again so I nodded and turned to go again.

"And could you show up about half an hour early every week in case I need help with the roster, or someone forgets his shin guards or jersey or something else like that?" There was a pitiful, pleading look on his face.

"Sure, no big deal," I replied. This time I didn't even contemplate shaking his hand, and the smile had evaporated from my face. I just nodded and turned to go once more. (I was starting to get dizzy from all the abrupt turnarounds.)

"Oh, and one more thing. If you could type up a list of all the kids' names and phone numbers and get it to me by the next practice I'd sure appreciate it," he hollered after me.

"I'll try," was all he got in response—no hand shaking, no smile, not even a nod—as I turned to go for the fourth time.

"Wait a sec, I almost forgot about the fund-raiser and picture day. Oh, and we need to get trophies; and there's always an end-of-the-season picnic, and . . ."

I was way out of earshot and not about to turn around.

What had I gotten myself into? I realized I should have checked out the obligations of being a team mom long before I volunteered. I felt overwhelmed and somewhat used.

I remembered having the same feeling several years before—just a few days after my honeymoon had ended. My brand new husband and I had each completed a long day of school and work. As I crossed the threshold that evening, my darling husband had the audacity to ask me what I was planning to make for dinner.

"Wait a minute!" I had retorted. "I remember promising to love, honor, and cherish you. I don't remember promising to cook for you!"

But a slow realization that there was some kind of hidden agenda I hadn't counted on began to dawn on me. There was a lot more to being a wife than was implicated by a simple "I do!"

The same feeling had recurred a few years later when my husband and I proudly (and ignorantly) carried our first baby boy home in our arms. We were suddenly introduced to parenthood. After the second sleepless night, we peered at each other through blood-shot eyes and asked, "What have we gotten ourselves into?" Nobody had mentioned that parenting would be quite so tiring—or so permanent.

I decided to stick it out as the team mom that year, just as I have stuck out being a wife, a mother, and the countless other volunteer roles I have placed myself in over the years. I have many happy memories (and some extra shin guards in the closet) to prove it.

My prayer for today:

Please, Lord, give me wisdom and discernment concerning the many tasks that are set before me every day. I need to be careful not to over-schedule my life. Please help me learn to be selective. With Your guidance, may I become involved in the activities that will bring You the most glory. As I assume responsibilities, help my attitude and my actions to be wholehearted and pleasing to You. Give me a *diligent* heart today, dear God, one that works hard to bring You honor through all my commitments.

Amen.

Want It?
Work for It!

*He who gathers crops in summer is a wise son, but
he who sleeps during harvest is a disgraceful son.*

Proverbs 10:5

Somehow, my thirteen-year-old son has come up with the
mistaken notion that summer vacations are meant to be fun.
He views his two-month break from school as a reward—a
prize for having completed a few months of conjugating verbs
and multiplying fractions.

Besides staying in bed until noon, he feels that his reward
should include: hours of playing baseball, swimming whenever
he pleases, watching every movie that has been released in the
past five years, planning trips to all the theme parks in
Florida, and playing video games with the neighbor until his
fingers are too sore to vacuum his room or wash the car.

He wants to ride a roller coaster, boogie board at the beach, and raise his own reptile. Nowhere does folding the laundry, doing the dishes, or mowing the lawn fit into his idea of summertime fun.

I think he fails to understand the history and true intent of summer vacation. Originally, the very purpose of a break from school was to provide *parents* with a respite. Children were released from their academic pursuits so they could help with the planting, weeding, and harvesting of summer crops. In the "olden days," mental work gave way only to concentrated physical labor. As a result, children actually looked forward to the fall and the subsequent resumption of school activities.

Somehow over the years, we have mistakenly taught our kids that summer vacations were designed for *their* pleasure. We've led them to believe that summer (indeed all of life) was meant to be a blast. Early in life they learned to eat their meals at colorful restaurants with gigantic playgrounds, grabbing bites between trips down long, curvy slides. They learned to recite the alphabet accompanied by loud rhythmic songs and the exploits of funky cartoon characters. They visited the dentist in an office designed like a giant, floating spaceship, where the hygienists dressed as aliens.

It's no wonder that by the time they become teenagers, our children have turned the word "party" into a verb. A party is no longer a special occasion. It's the way we've taught them to live.

Delayed gratification is a foreign concept to Generation Next. We've failed to teach them to work for what they desire in life. And we've certainly not taught them to share what they have been so freely given with those less fortunate than they are.

The same kids who begged for toy vacuums and play lawn mowers (which we no doubt provided) when they were young, won't be caught dead pushing real ones as teenagers—especially on *their* summer vacation.

I think it's time we did away with "ouchless" band-aids and "no more tears" shampoo. Our kids need to know that real life stings once in a while—and that lawn mowers weren't created just to produce pretty bubbles. We need to stop overprotecting and underexpecting. We need to let our children know that the best things in life often come with a price.

Recently we instituted a "work for fun" policy at our house. If you want to go to the beach, first you have to wax

the car. Sure you can play a video game—if your bed is made and the garbage has been taken out. And today you can stay in bed as long as you want . . . since you helped clean the garage all day yesterday.

Do you know what we've discovered? Our teenager is beginning to appreciate some of the extra pleasures in life rather than expecting them. Even cleaning the rain gutters can be fun if we make it a family project—and sometimes tack on a trip to Disney World!

My prayer for today:

Lord, I want my children to be wise in Your sight. I want them to grow to be young men who know the value of hard work and consistent effort. I admit that sometimes it is much easier to do the tasks myself rather than assign and oversee them. But help me care enough about my children's development that I am willing to endure momentary conflicts and complaints in order to impart wisdom. Give me a *teaching* heart, dear God, one that will cultivate the right attributes in the lives of my children.

Amen.

Whose Way?

There is a way that seems right to a man,
but in the end it leads to death.

Proverbs 14:12

"Mom, I figured out how it all works," Jonathan boldly stated one afternoon. He stared wisely out into the universe and revealed the deep knowledge which had just been generated somewhere deep within his five-year-old brain.

"It's like we live on this big round ball. The sun goes round and round and round us while we stay on our ball."

His left fist became the earth, and his right hand circled it clumsily as he demonstrated the path of the sun. His tongue protruded sideways from between his teeth as he illustrated for me, making his words somewhat difficult to understand. But I hung in there.

"When the sun is on the side where we are," he garbled, "then we have lots of light. That's when it's day." His right hand continued to circle his left. "When it's not on our side, then it's dark." He looked up. "That's night!" he added succinctly, thinking I might be having trouble keeping up.

He smugly pressed his lips together (his tongue was back in his mouth by now) and gave a self-satisfied little nod indicating that the discourse of his newly acquired knowledge was complete, even though his hands kept gyrating.

"Jonathan, that is so clever!" I enthusiastically encouraged. "It really does work almost like that!"

I recognized that this was one of those infrequent moments of true vulnerability in learning, a moment when his mind was open to real understanding, so I didn't want to blow him away with the fact that he was dead wrong.

"Let me show you how it really works!"

I grabbed the revolving hand and held it still. "The sun is the thing that actually stands still," I explained. "And the big round ball that we live on goes round and round it."

He let me manipulate his left hand circuitously around his right. I was doing so well, I decided to continue.

"And, guess what! The ball, which is our Earth, spins as it goes around the sun, and that's what makes the light and the dark. See?" I tried to demonstrate.

"Oops. Let's get a tennis ball to be the earth," I suggested as I screwed his hand back on.

I was really into this. I gathered a tennis ball, a flashlight, the globe, and some ping-pong balls; and I demonstrated until I was sure that he knew more than any other child his age about how our planet (and our whole solar system for that matter) revolves, rotates, and reflects. I even included such things as the tilted axis, seasons, moons, and tides.

Jonathan sat there silently, absorbing it all. When I had finally used up all my information, I sat back and smiled. "Isn't it neat how God put everything together, Jonathan? Everything works so well! What do you think of it?"

Long silence. Deep contemplation on his part.

"Well . . . I guess God's way would work," he finally responded. "But I like my way a whole lot better!"

Long silence. Deep contemplation on my part.

"Don't we all, Jonathan. That's the problem on this earth. We all like our own way better!"

My prayer for today:

I know that Your ways are right, Lord, and I know that they are the very best. I know that following them will lead to peace and joy and fellowship with You. So why do I so often try to do things my own way? My response to many situations is as immature as that of a five-year-old insisting he could run the universe. Help me choose to obey and follow You in paths that lead to life. Give me a *submissive* heart, dear God, one that wants to live life Your way.

Amen.

Work Some Encouragement

---

*Therefore encourage one another
and build each other up.*

1 Thessalonians 5:11

At one time in our lives, when our legs felt young and our energy seemed boundless, my husband and I jogged together for about an hour each evening. Actually we didn't really jog together. We jogged separately, but we were still together. It's hard to explain, but I guess I'd better try now that I've gotten myself into this.

You see, at that time we lived in a planned community just south of Atlanta. It was a beautiful city with miles of jogging paths. They wound their way through quiet woods, skirted a man-made lake, passed over a busy highway, and traversed alongside the local golf course. Since the paths

connected residents with everything from a grocery store to a recreation center, and since golf carts were permitted on the jogging paths, we decided to invest in one as our second vehicle. It was a thrifty idea for a young, growing family. We used it constantly and even traveled to church in our cart on more than one occasion.

We had the cart rigged with a special back seat, replacing the normal club holders. Many evenings we strapped on toddler and baby seats, and the whole family spent a healthy, happy evening in the fresh air. One of us drove while the other jogged. When the jogger's legs or lungs grew weary, we switched. (Now can you understand how we were able to jog separately yet still be together?)

Anyway, about three months into this routine, my husband decided he would enter a 10K road race. This required extra practice miles on his part. One evening, as he was pushing for some additional distance, his legs slowed down. Each step he took seemed heavier than the last, each breath more labored, until it appeared that he was about to collapse.

"Let's help Daddy out," I challenged my two-year-old. "Let's give him some words of encouragement."

Always literal-minded, our toddler began to yell from the back seat of the golf cart, "Work some encouragement, Daddy! Work some encouragement!"

"No, honey—I said *words* of encouragement. We need to give Daddy some *words* of encouragement."

I was wasting my breath. The phrase had already stuck in his two-year-old brain. "Work some encouragement!" he kept yelling. "You can do it, Dad. Work some encouragement!"

It wasn't exactly what I had in mind, but it worked. Dad immediately perked up (after almost choking with laughter) and sprinted on home.

From then on, when anyone in our family has needed a little extra boost in their endeavors, someone else has been there to yell, "Work some encouragement! You can do it, Son (or Mom, or Granny). Work some encouragement!"

It has been whispered with a wink as a son was about to take the stage in his very first performance (a much dreaded role as Abraham Lincoln). It has been yelled at the ball field when a son has pitched his way to a 3-0 count or gone 0-2 as a batter. It has been written on a note and stuck in Mom's purse when she was about to address a large, grown-up audience.

It's our special way of saying, "Hey, hang in there. You're doing great. We're right here with you, and we know you can do it!"

It hasn't solved all of life's dilemmas, but it has produced a lot of courageous performances and evoked many thankful smiles.

My prayer for today:

You've given us family and friends, Lord, so that we can help each other along the pathways of this life. It is our God-given responsibility to build each other up. You never intended for us to tear each other down. Yet so many times, in so many ways, our words and actions are detrimental. Let the words that come out of my mouth today be ones that encourage and rebuild the esteem of those around me. Help me to see someone grow before my eyes today as I build them up in their faith and their esteem. Give me an *encouraging* heart, dear God.

Amen.

A Different Kind of Poverty Level

Command those who are rich in this present world not to be arrogant nor to put their hope in wealth, which is so uncertain, but to put their hope in God, who richly provides us with everything for our enjoyment. Command them to do good, to be rich in good deeds, and to be generous and willing to share.

1 Timothy 6:17-18

Toby is an outdoor dog. He lives in our big, fenced-in back yard all day (unless it's too cold or rainy), and he sleeps on the porch next to our cat at night. He is a wonderful

eighty-five pounds worth of German shepherd and yellow lab we rescued from the SPCA a few Christmases ago.

Toby is everything a boy ever wanted in a dog (and I think each one of our four sons supplies everything a dog ever desired in a boy). He's a great companion. He loves to jump on the trampoline, go for long walks, or fetch a ball. Plus he can catch a Frisbee just like the dogs in the commercials do.

When the weather gets cold—about three days a year here in central Florida—Toby snuggles up in a big bedspread on the carpeted part of the porch, while the cat curls itself into a basket lined with towels. Toby won't allow the cat on his bedspread, but they manage to stay close enough to keep each other warm.

Well, not long ago, the weather suddenly turned very cold. I hurried home from a meeting I had attended to let Toby in on the porch. I immediately went to the garage to retrieve his bedspread from the cupboard where we stored it. But it wasn't there. Then I recalled that it had become so dilapidated I had discarded it after the last cold snap.

I wasn't sure what to do. I didn't have another spread or blanket available for "dog use," and I certainly didn't want to spend money on a new one just for canine creature comforts. I know he's part of the family and all, but thirty bucks for one night's warmth seemed to be a little much.

Finally, after checking several department stores, I decided that the only solution was to try a thrift shop. Toby certainly didn't need a brand new bedspread to nestle in. So off I went to the Salvation Army thrift store to see if they had any in stock. I felt strange driving up in my nice van—there were so many disintegrating vehicles parked out front. I felt even stranger when I realized that I was still very dressed up from my meeting. I didn't feel like I belonged. But since I was already there, I decided to pursue my quest.

Sure enough there was a whole section of blankets and spreads at the very back of the store. I joined an elderly, little man who was digging through the stock. I said a polite "Hello. How are you?" and without waiting for a reply blabbed my way right into an explanation of why I was in that store at that time, looking through that bin with him. "So you see, I really need to get a spread for my dog so he doesn't get too cold."

I looked up and the little man was staring at me like I was some kind of fool—and indeed I was. From the clothes on his back and the shoes on his feet, that weather-worn, world-weary gentleman looked just about as poor as any human could look and still maintain his dignity. He turned and walked away.

There I had stood, trying to explain my problems and presence in a thrift store to a poor, elderly gentleman who had far greater adversities of his own. I had been so busy trying to adjust my image and explain my actions that I had not taken the time to really look at him—a person who could have used God's love demonstrated through me in any number of ways.

No, it wasn't my image that needed adjusting that day. It was my heart. Poverty comes in many different forms. Some are more visible than others.

My prayer for today:

Lord, sometimes I get things so confused. I know that You are interested in adjusting my attitude, yet I spend so

much time and energy adjusting my image. I guess I'm afraid of being seen as vulnerable in some way. This would not be a problem if I learned to focus on others rather than myself. Take away my agendas and replace them with Your purposes. Make me rich in those things that count for eternity. Give me a *sensitive* heart, dear God, one that is willing to care and share.

Amen.

A Stranger in the Family

I stood quietly outside the slightly cracked door as I often
did after tucking my little ones into bed. I loved to hear the
late night philosophical conversations that poured forth from
the minds and hearts of my little men as they discussed the
events of their day and their plans for tomorrow.

It seemed that every time the lights went out, some sort
of special insight and wisdom turned on. Brain waves, which
had been occupied all day with figuring out effective means
of extracting baseballs from gutters and practical ways to
construct indestructible forts, were suddenly free to frolic in
fields of fantasy and fly off into the future.

This particular day had been a special one. A police officer had visited Zach's kindergarten class. The children had listened to police stories and examined police paraphernalia for over an hour. Zach was one of the "lucky" ones who got to be handcuffed to his desk!

Just before he left to go back on patrol, the police officer read the class a story. It was titled *Betsy and Bill and the Nice Bad Man*. It was a very exciting story. Each of the children had been given his very own copy of the large, twenty-page text with the bright, colorful pictures to take home and read with his or her parents.

Between the time Zach arrived home from school and bedtime, we read the story at least five times. Three-year-old Matt was fascinated with it. He paged through it, pouring over the pictures, at least a dozen more times on his own.

It was a story about two children who walked to and from their neighborhood elementary school every day. On the way home one day, they were approached by a very nice man in a big, red car. He offered them some candy. Bill was easily lured by the stranger. Betsy, following a few yards behind, watched in horror as her brother was pulled into the car and whisked away.

Fortunately, the author stationed a police officer nearby. He intervened before anything tragic could happen, and everyone lived happily ever after, having learned a very valuable lesson: *You must never talk to strangers*—especially if they offer you candy.

The conversation that night, as I stood quietly in the hall, centered around the policeman's visit to school and the story he had shared with the students. After a short discussion, Zach concluded, "Policemen wear neat stuff and do lots of good things. They help little kids like us all the time. I think I'm going to be a policeman when I grow up."

I smiled, as any proud mother would have.

"Not me!" piped up my three-year-old. "Being a pawiceman is too much hawd wook!" he added.

There was silence for a few minutes, then very thoughtfully he added, "I think I'm just going to be a stwanja when I gwow up. Then I can just dwive awound in a big wed caw and give candy to wittle childwen."

Oops! Somehow MattE had missed the point of the story. Even though he had been through the story dozens of times,

his immature little mind was not able to comprehend the message.

"We'll have to try that story again in a few years," I promised myself.

Well, MattE just turned twenty the other day, and all the kids in the neighborhood adore him—especially when he gives them candy. Actually, we're extremely proud of how he has grown up. But no matter how mature he becomes, we'll probably never allow him to drive a big, red car!

My prayer for today:

Lord, we smile at the cute immaturity of our children. They provide us with many fond memories of their growing-up years. But we would be devastated if our children failed to develop and remained immature youngsters all their lives. Help me realize that the same is true of my spiritual life. I don't want to remain underdeveloped as a believer. Instead I want to please You with my progress. Show me from Your Word today an area in which I need to grow. Then teach me ways to make the changes in my life that will produce maturity. Give me a *continually developing* heart, dear God.

Amen.

A Time to Heal

Be devoted to one another in brotherly love.
Honor one another above yourselves.

Romans 12:10

Our sons are close in age, and close in their relationships
to one another. So when Zach left home almost three years
ago and headed out on his own (he and about a million other
teenage refugees!) into the world of college life, we figured it
might be hard on his brothers. We anticipated it would take
several months for them to adjust to his absence—particularly
Jonathan, the youngest, who always teamed up with him in
brotherly competitions (both sports and spats).

However, no sooner had Zach's overstuffed car backed
out of the driveway than Jonathan disappeared inside with
one goal in mind—to take over his brother's mostly vacated

room. Leftover shoes, ratty sweatshirts, and broken baseball equipment wound up in the hall as Jonathan stashed his own stuff in its place.

Finally, after twelve years of scrunching and sharing, he had a room to himself! Plus, he still had two brothers left at home to play with and pick on him. Could life get any sweeter?

Last year our second son exported himself to the college world. Once again, it wasn't the fact that MattE was departing forever that created a poignant moment for Jonathan. It was the fact that he now had two whole rooms to himself, one to live in and one to store his junk in! He could barely contain his glee.

Of course, there was yet another brother at home, who happened to be quite content inhabiting just one room, and who was more than willing to cart Jonathan around town and wrestle with him. Jonathan was happier than a two-tongued frog in a swamp full of dragonflies!

However, recently we began to wonder how he will ever handle things when Ben, who is three years older and the only brother left at home, chooses to amble out of our world

into his own. (If you know Ben, you understand that he doesn't walk or run or ride. He ambles.)

So today, after a particularly brotherly episode involving the two of them—which included a lot of laughing and punching and mimicking and tormenting, and ended with Jonathan's head accidentally crashing into an overhanging cupboard—I asked Jonathan what on earth he intended to do when his last brother left home.

Without a moment's hesitation he replied, "Heal!"

We all burst out laughing.

It's true that as the baby of the family Jonathan has not only been well-loved, he has been "well-handled" by his brothers. And sometimes the handling has been a little rough. At the age of three, his arm was accidentally broken when Ben took him out for a bike-riding lesson. At eleven, his leg snapped in two when he smashed into a chain link fence while shagging balls for Zach and MattE. And today his forehead received another large goose egg.

However, I have a feeling that three years of healing may be a little more than Jonathan's body requires. There will be a lot of empty time to occupy, and it may get lonely trying to

fend for himself. At some point, Jonathan is surely going to miss his brothers. (We have already noticed that he spends an inordinate amount of time bugging Ben in his room lately.) Besides, what use could he possibly have for a third bedroom?

My prayer for today:

As my children have grown I have often prayed, Lord, that You would instill in them a sense of camaraderie and closeness. I have prayed that they will be companions to each other all through their lives. As with all relationships there have been times of disagreement and disharmony. They don't always appreciate each other as I think they should. But thank You, Lord, for their underlying devotion and loyalty to each other. Help me be as committed to my brothers and sisters in Christ as my children are to each other. Don't let me abandon them when there are disagreements or hurt feelings. Let love and dedication prevail as I seek to regard them more highly than myself. Give me a *devoted* heart, dear God, one that seeks to honor my brothers and sisters in Christ more than I honor myself.

Amen.

A Game of Gopher Heads

"Martha, Martha," the Lord answered, "you are worried and upset about many things, but only one thing is needed. Mary has chosen what is better, and it will not be taken away from her."

Luke 10:41-42

Life is like a lot of things. Forrest Gump's momma insightfully observed that life is a lot like a box of chocolates, because "you never know what you're gonna get." Vince Lombardi, a former NFL head coach, decided that life is like a game of football. "You're either getting better or you're getting worse. You never stay the same."

Well, after making my own astute observations, I've decided that life is actually very much like a game of Gopher Heads.

Unless you frequent amusement arcades, you probably don't have a clue how to unravel the wisdom entwined within that statement. So let me try to explain. When you walk through the front door of a fun center (only because your child has decided to torture and bankrupt you by inviting ten of his wildest friends to his birthday celebration at such a location), usually one of the first games you encounter is called Gopher Heads. It is a big colorful table with about eight round holes carved in the top. It makes a great central meeting place and provides a wonderful vantage point from which to assure that none of the "partiers" scoots out before the cake and ice cream.

So after you have filled all the kids' pockets with jingling tokens, and find yourself completely abandoned, you usually end up sitting on a stool next to the table with the round holes. Bored, you begin to read the instructions under the Plexiglas sign.

It informs you that the holes in the table are actually gopher holes. (Some versions use alligators or chipmunks, but it really doesn't matter. The concept is the same.) A big, cushioned mallet is dangling from the table. You are instructed to insert a token into the table, grab the mallet,

and start bopping gophers on the head as they pop up out of the holes. Your task is to bop as many as you can before they pop back into their hiding holes.

Easy enough, right? So when none of the kids is looking, you decide to play. You insert an extra token you find in your pocketbook, grab the mallet, and within a few seconds knock a gopher silly before it can disappear back into the depths of the game board.

Aha! This is great! Not only is this a game you can handle (as opposed to electronic snow skiing), but there is also a macabre joy in smacking little rodents as they jeer at you.

However, as soon as you bop one, out pops another, then another, and another. The faster you bop, the faster they pop. And once bopped, they don't necessarily stay bopped! They come up jeering again and again, until finally you are swinging wildly and randomly just trying to hit anything that might get in the way of the mallet. You finish the game out of breath and totally frustrated. But for some reason, as soon as it's over, you insert another token!

Doesn't this sound a little bit like life? Maybe yours isn't as hectic as mine, but it seems like all I do most days is bop

gophers. As soon as I get one gopher under control, out pops another, then another, and another.

It's usually my own fault. I'm the one who chooses to play the gopher game. Instead of sticking tokens into a slot, I stick events and obligations onto my calendar. At first everything is fine, but by the end of most days, I'm swinging wildly and randomly, just hoping to stay in the game. There are so many gophers that there is no way to keep them all under control at one time.

I've finally decided that the only solution is to say "No!" I must learn to gracefully turn down the people who constantly try to add gophers to my life. They're just going to have to give those gophers to someone else—and let them bop for a while!

My prayer for today:

Too often, Lord, I find myself so busy that I don't even have time to talk to You. I know that You never meant life to be this hectic! Please help me slow down. Help me learn to say "no" to activities that take me away from You or my

husband or my children. Give me the wisdom to establish the priorities You intended for my life. Strengthen my commitment to them so I don't miss the treasures that You have for me. Give me an *uncluttered* heart, dear God, one that seeks to include only the things that You think are important.

Amen.

Ben Grows Up—His Own Way

My son, preserve sound judgment and discernment,
do not let them out of your sight; they will be life for
you, an ornament to grace your neck.
Then you will go on your way in safety,
and your foot will not stumble.

Proverbs 3:21-23

Our third son is now a 6-foot 4-inch high school senior who is about to graduate. I don't know which surprises us more—the fact that he is so tall (and still growing!) or the fact that he actually passed enough grades to graduate from high school!

There has never been any question that Ben was smart enough to make it through school. He's probably smarter than all the rest of us put together. At times, however, there were questions about whether he would ever choose to apply his brilliance to textbook material or if he would wind up making his living as a stand-up comedian.

Ben has never done anything the conventional way. A huge end-of-the-year history project last year was not presented on a display board like everyone else's. His was displayed in boxes stacked on their sides and piled like a pyramid. (He ended up with the highest grade. For once a teacher appreciated his non-conformist attitude!) Most of his yearbook picture proofs came back with him neatly attired in a tuxedo, wearing his baseball cap!

He has never comprehended the need to adhere to strict MLA term paper format when doing a research paper. He has trouble with rules like: One must place all his parenthetical citations within a closing quotation mark but preceding the sentence punctuation.

"Who cares as long as I get my point across?!" he wants to know. And where and when on earth will he ever need to know how to solve geometric logarithms in real life, he

questioned last year. His teacher came up with some reply. I sure couldn't!

Often we have wished he would be more like the other kids. We've wanted him to conform like most of them, and play the learning game the way the teachers like it played.

But through the years, Ben has hung in there, with us hanging on right beside him. And here he is—a senior well on the way to graduation with what actually has turned out to be a very acceptable GPA! We have come to appreciate his unique style and wonderful sense of humor—and he has learned to adapt them into conformity with most school rules and parental regulations.

For instance, last semester when several of Ben's macho senior friends were taunted by underclassmen in the senior lounge and ended up hanging them by their britches from the weight machines, Ben chose not to participate. (He didn't help any of the underclassmen down, but, hey, at least he didn't hang any of them up resulting in a one-day suspension!)

And not long ago when most of his classmates chose to hold a wild shindig while one set of parents was out of town,

Ben chose not to attend! Instead he spent the night with a quiet friend on the other side of town.

Come to think of it, we're awfully glad he doesn't always conform like most kids do! We're glad he doesn't play the same games that many of them are playing. Ben has almost always shown sound judgment and discernment—despite the interference of his mom and dad.

And you know, he's absolutely right. I don't know a single person who has ever had to solve a geometric logarithm since his or her junior year in high school!

My prayer for today:

Thank You, Lord, for the individuality of my children. You have created each one differently, with his own special personality and unique set of gifts. Yet, naively I sometimes find myself forcing these wonderful, God-formed creatures into molds designed by society. I pray that each of my children will develop sound judgment and discernment and that, above all else, they will bring You joy and glory. Please keep them from stumbling along the way to maturity. Give me a *peaceful* heart, dear God, as I allow You to work in my children's lives.

Amen.

Furniture Doesn't Last Forever

We could be sitting on a comfortable, new couch in our family room with cups of cappuccino carefully poised on coasters at the edge of a brightly polished, new coffee table right now, but we're not.

We would love to take you out in the back yard a little later, when the temperature cools down, and enjoy the evening grilling chicken and watching the sunset from our newly renovated deck, but we won't.

That's because we never saved quite enough money to refurbish the dilapidated sectional and replace the broken coffee table in the family room; and we never quite got around to refinishing the creaky, old deck out back this summer like we had planned.

Although we promised ourselves early in May that both jobs would be accomplished by the time autumn rolled around, we just didn't get them done. Labor Day weekend would have been the perfect time, with all the summer clearance sales and the extra time off from school and work, but we opted instead for one more annual trip to the beach with all four of our sons.

We realized that this might be the last year our whole family would be able to converge at New Smyrna Beach to enjoy the Labor Day vacation together, as we have at the end of each summer for the past sixteen years. So we elected to spend our money on a weekend rental, and we chose to spend our time just being together.

We figured that our four sons would remember boogie boarding the breakers; taking long walks on the cool, soft

141

sand; playing flag football with newfound friends; watching moonlight magic on the waves; (and let's not forget competing in the annual Diaz brothers' wiffle ball competition) far more dearly than they would ever recall a comfortable new couch or a solid new deck.

They'll never forget scurrying after sand fleas, building castles with moats, and diving into the surf after wayward Frisbees. These are annual traditions. Even as young adults, they insist on evening Slurpees at the nearby 7-Eleven, and the yearly trip to Inlet Charlie's to look over the 50 percent sale on all swimsuits and the latest fashions in surfboards. Hopefully, they'll always cherish the precious time spent evaluating the past year and sharing and praying for each other.

Yes, we could have skipped these sentimental memories, and right now we would be seated on a new settee arranging glossy magazines on its accompanying coffee table to make room for the cappuccino. We could have foregone the fun and fashioned ourselves a brand new deck overlooking the azaleas in our back yard.

Yet as we sit on the tattered couch, holding our mugs on our laps and looking out over the warped and peeling deck, our hearts are happy—happy for all the memories that we did choose to spend our money on; happy for all the things we accomplished instead. The way we figure it, new couches quickly grow old, and old couches soon have to be replaced. (It's the same

with wooden decks.) But the family memories we made just a few weeks ago will never become outdated. They will never need to be replaced. They will probably grow more precious with time. Sure, they might fade a little and the details might get somewhat rumpled. (Which team really won the annual wiffle ball competition is already being hotly debated.) But just in case that happens, we've got most of them stored away in a picture album in the family room closet. I'll set it out on the coffee table for everyone to see—as soon as we get one!

My prayer for today:

Lord, when I start to complain about the things I don't have, would You please remind me of all the things that I do have: the great times that I've spent with friends and family, all the special places You've allowed me to go, and all the neat people that I've been privileged to meet. You have provided me with so many rich experiences and filled my life with so much intangible joy. Thank You! Don't ever let me become so shallow that I begin to think that tangible things could make me any happier than my relationship with You already does. Give me a *wisely invested* heart, dear God, one that knows where true treasures can be found.

Amen.

Cats Can't Baby-sit

May the LORD *make you increase, both you and your children. May you be blessed by the* LORD*, the Maker of heaven and earth.*

Psalm 115:14-15

It was a Tuesday evening. The baseball team had just won a huge game. Everyone on the team was jumping around, giving each other high five's—everyone except my fifteen-year-old, that is. He approached me with a downcast, forlorn look on his face.

"What's the matter?" I needed to know. "Why aren't you excited? Your team just won!"

"Yeah, but I also just failed my fifth period exploratory wheel class," he mumbled dejectedly. "I left my stupid 'egg kids' home without a baby-sitter!"

I didn't have a clue what he was talking about. I wondered if the hit he had taken when he slid into base during the second inning had scrambled his brains.

"What on earth is an egg kid?" I demanded.

He filled me in. Apparently at school that day each student had been given an egg. For three days they were to be responsible for it as though it was a real child. They were to treat it gently and take it with them wherever they went. The eggs had come with little felt caps and silly felt-tip smiles. Much to his chagrin, the only set of twins had been placed in my son's custodial care.

He had brought his egg babies home that afternoon in a little basket filled with Easter grass and immediately shoved them in the fridge. The last place he ever expected to run into his teacher was at the ball field that night. But there she was, and sometime around the sixth inning, she managed to ask him through the dugout fence where his egg twins were. She let him know in no uncertain terms that, "Home, chillin' in the fridge," was not an acceptable answer.

"You weren't really serious, were you?" he asked. "You didn't *really* expect me to bring eggs with faces on them to the ball field? Besides, they're a whole lot safer in the fridge

146

than they would be out here. Do you know what a foul ball can do to an egg?" he quickly reasoned.

His teacher wasn't the least bit amused by his logic. "It's considered child abuse to leave your babies unattended," she responded quite seriously. "I'll have to mark your grade way down!"

"Child abuse! That's ridiculous!" He was more than a little perturbed. "Anyway, I didn't leave them home unattended. The cat is taking care of them."

She shook her head. "I'm afraid cats can't function as baby-sitters," she responded quite curtly.

"Hey, if eggs can be babies, why can't cats be baby-sitters?" His argument was clever, but she didn't buy it.

Consequently, those egg babies got shoved in a shoe box, crammed into his backpack, and carried around with him for the better part of two days in an effort to salvage his grade.

"Egg kids are a real pain," he grumbled quite often. "You can't just dump them somewhere. You've got to drag them with you wherever you go!"

"I know the feeling," I empathized sarcastically. "Wait 'til you have to feed them, make them clean up their rooms, and be sure they get their homework done," I added as I rolled my eyes.

My son was thrilled when Thursday rolled around. Joyfully, he turned his egg kids back in. (One had cracked its skull somehow in the shoe box. Fortunately they were hard-boiled.) Somehow he managed to survive the assignment, and I think he might have learned a thing or two in the process.

I considered trying to explain to him how he really would have gotten used to his egg babies if he had let them hang around a little longer; how taking care of them could have actually brought him joy; how his "children" could have become a vital and fun part of his life; and how one day he might actually consider them a tremendous blessing—but I knew he wasn't ready to understand.

So I explained it all to the cat. He might not be a good sitter, but he's a great listener.

My prayer for today:

Lord, You have truly blessed me by giving me children. Help me to be able to convey this attitude of honor and joy to them today. Help them know how privileged I feel that You, the Maker of Heaven and Earth, decided to entrust me with their care. Sometimes the task is challenging, but You

knew that with Your help I could meet the challenge. May the attitudes I convey to my children cause them to look forward to the task of parenting in the future. May my actions prepare them for the challenges they face ahead. Give me a *committed* heart, dear God, one that rejoices and labors diligently in the task You have set before me.

Amen.

Deception in the Perception

Now we see but a poor reflection as in a mirror;
then we shall see face to face. Now I know in part;
then I shall know fully, even as I am fully known.

1 Corinthians 13:12

Back in the days when our local airport ran commuter
flights to Tampa and Orlando, my husband often took the
Friday afternoon flight out of town on his way to a speaking
engagement. Dropping him off became almost a weekly
family event. All four children, plus their strollers and toys,
would pile into the station wagon with Mom and Dad, and
we would head to the airport.

We dropped Dad at the lobby door, then parked at the far
end of the parking lot where we could best watch his plane

take off. While we waited, we played with our footballs and frisbees and had a little snack. (We never knew quite how long he would be delayed, but we were prepared!)

As the plane roared down the runway, the kids climbed on top of the station wagon and waved and yelled "good-bye" to Dad—all except our three-year-old. He was always very involved in the activity up until that point; but suddenly, as the plane took off, he turned into a quiet little statue. Instead of waving and carrying on like the rest of us, he just stood on the ground quietly staring at the departing plane. With glazed eyes he gazed into the horizon watching the speck become smaller and smaller until it completely disappeared. I had to bodily pick him up and place him in his car seat for the ride home. Once we pulled into the driveway, his true, wild nature returned almost as abruptly as it had disappeared.

Again there would be a total change in his demeanor when we received a call from the airport and rushed off to pick up Dad on Sunday evening. Like a silent zombie, he would stare at his dad as he exited from the lobby. "You're big!" he once exclaimed as his dad tossed him in the air. We laughed and agreed, "Yeah, Dad is pretty big!"

Then came the special day when we all got to go to the big airport in Tampa, get on an airplane with Dad, and fly to a conference in Texas. Everyone was excited—except our three-year-old. He asked strange questions while we packed our suitcases, "Will my clothes still fit me when I'm in the airplane?" and "Does it hurt to be little?"

He walked like a zombie on the way to the airport, never uttering a word. He silently held my hand and tiptoed beside me as we made our way to the gate. Finally it was time to get on board. There was pure excitement as we headed down the tunnel to the plane—except for child number three. His eyes were wide, and his lips were shut tight. We jockeyed for the best seats, got out the least noisy toys, and buckled up for takeoff.

"Here we go!" one of the boys shrieked as we headed down the runway. Silence from our three-year-old. "Look, we're in the clouds!" another child was ecstatic. Not a peep from child number three. "Go, go, go!" yelled the baby. Our three-year-old sat as still as a stone.

Finally, he reached over and pulled my sleeve. In a small shaky voice he asked, "Mommy, when do we get real little?"

Seeing my puzzled expression, he tried to explain. "You know, like Daddy does when he gets on an airplane and it goes in the sky. He gets real little! When does that happen to us?"

Suddenly I understood his whole airport dilemma. He had absolutely no concept of depth perception—at least when it came to airplanes taking off. He had seen them shrink before his very eyes, diminishing everything within them, including Dad. He obviously concluded that he was about to be reduced to the size of a mosquito!

It took a lot of explaining, but finally he seemed to comprehend. He decided that airplanes were really cool after all. Several times I had to quiet him down on the trip as he laughed and played with his brothers.

I realized then that reality is not always as we perceive it, even when we see it with our very own eyes! Only God can see the total picture in all its proper dimensions.

My prayer for today:

I know, Lord, that many times my perception is warped as I try to analyze and justify events in my life. You must shake Your head in disbelief at some of my misconceptions, false assumptions, and rationalizations. Help me take more time to

153

look at life through Your Word and Your eyes and less time trying to squint at it through my own eyes. I want to perceive situations the same way You do. Give me an *unclouded* heart, dear God, one that looks at life with Your clarity.

Amen.

Filling the Right Basket

So then, just as you received Christ Jesus as Lord,
continue to live in him, rooted and built up in him,
strengthened in the faith as you were taught,
and overflowing with thankfulness.

Colossians 2:6-7

Baskets of various shapes and sizes are strategically strewn around our house. Some are decorative, like the expensive, cane-woven one that enhances a large, leafy plant in the corner of the living room and the delicate ribboned baskets that sport colorful, silk arrangements. Some are practical, like the square basket that attempts to corral the mail on my desk and the fruit basket that sits on the kitchen counter.

But most of the baskets serve only one purpose. They exist to control the clutter and chaos of a place that houses

four children. One such basket holds cars and trucks of all shapes and sizes. Several hold crayons and pens and pencils. There's one for video game equipment, one for loose change, and even one for everything else that has no place to go. What would I do without baskets?

The other day, as I was tossing abandoned shoes into a shoe basket and scattered books into a book basket, I came across a tiny angel that belonged in an old pop-up book of Jonathan's. Somehow it had escaped from the confines of its paper paradise, and, trumpet still in hand, lay prone on the living room floor. It reminded me of a story I had been told when I was a small child, a story about two angels and two baskets.

As the story goes, it was the job of these two heavenly angels to collect all the prayers of the inhabitants of earth. So every evening, sometime before midnight, they flew to earth, each holding a basket. One angel carried a basket labeled "Gimme." The other angel's basket was marked "Thank You."

Every night when they returned to heaven after completing their earthly chores, it was the same story. The Gimme angel had a basket so full that it was overflowing. It took every ounce of her angelic strength to lift the load from cloud to cloud and place it before the angelic hosts in

heaven. They immediately set to work, scurrying around, sorting and sifting the pleas of the frail humans below.

The Thank-You angel's basket, on the other hand, was virtually empty. She quickly flew through the golden gates and hid her basket so that no other angelic beings could see how ungrateful human beings are. She felt dejected and disgraced. I think she might have even cried.

My childhood prayers changed radically after hearing this story. Every night I worked diligently to fill the basket of the Thank-You angel. I was careful not to utter a word that could possibly wind up in the Gimme angel's stash. Even if I wanted something, I'd figure out a way to thank God that I didn't have it, so the Thank-You angel could get credit. (Secretly I hoped that God in His infinite wisdom would see fit, since I was such a thankful being, to bestow on me a new baby sister, or whatever it was I had just thanked Him for not having. He seldom did—He knew better—but I was okay with that. I could be happy as long as I thought the Thank-You angel had a little joy in her life.)

Over the years my angel images faded. Somewhere along the path of life I learned that, just as Santas don't deliver packages through chimneys and Easter Bunnies don't hide

eggs in bushes, angels don't collect prayers in baskets. And my Thank-You prayers subsided.

As I held the tiny paper angel in my hand remembering that story from my youth, I glanced around the room. I saw the overflowing contents of all my many baskets. I bowed my head. I had one more basket to fill before my work was done.

My prayer for today:

Thank You, Lord, for all the things in life that I take for granted every day. Thank You for warm water in my shower and cool water to quench my thirst. Thank You for flowers along my pathways and birds that sing their songs each new morning. Thank You for the life-giving sun and the rain-producing clouds and for shade trees, which benefit from both. Thank You for a place I can call home and a bed where I can lay my weary body. Thank You for my family and friends and the many strangers who add new dimensions to my life every day. Thank You for all the times You have put up with my selfishness. Give me a truly *thankful* heart every day, dear God, one that overflows with gratitude and praise.

Amen.

Finer Than a Fixer

If the whole body were an eye, where would the sense of hearing be? If the whole body were an ear, where would the sense of smell be? But in fact God has arranged the parts in the body, every one of them, just as he wanted them to be.

1 Corinthians 12:17-18

Our family room furniture has definitely seen better days. The large sectional and its matching recliner have been bounced from, sat upon, slept on, and eaten on by more teenagers than you can pack into a movie theater on a Friday night.

Somehow during the progress of one of our parties, the reclining chair was broken. It became totally stuck in the down

position, making it very difficult to get into and even more difficult to get back out of. Talk about "laid back"! All anyone can do in such a position is enjoy a great view of one's own feet. (It's rather difficult to carry on a serious conversation when you have to constantly peek through your shoes.)

After checking out the interior rigging apparatus, we discovered that the board which supports the reclining mechanism had snapped in two. It appeared totally unsalvageable. It was doomed for the dumpster. So I had the kids carry it out to the curb.

My husband, however, had second thoughts. First of all, he realized that we didn't have the money to replace the recliner. Plus, after years of watching "fix it" shows on PBS, he figured this was a job he could handle. (If you were to ask him who he would most want to be like when he grows up, he'd probably say Norm Abram or Tim "The Toolman" Taylor. They are his heroes.)

Now mind you, my hubby has never fixed a faucet or salvaged a socket in his life!

Anyway, the recliner was rescued from the curb, and several trips were made to the hardware store. After many

hours, much sweat, and a little blood, the chair sat in a wonderful upright posture . . . until one of our sons plopped down in it.

I have to be truthful here. The recliner really was in a better state than it had been prior to Ed's attempt. It was a little less reclined than it had been before he started. You could actually see the television set over the tops of your shoes.

But Ed was discouraged. He truly felt that he should have been able to fix it. It was a blow to his male ego that the stupid thing didn't work like it was supposed to. No doubt Norm Abram would have had it working in less than an hour. And Tim Taylor would have had it working so powerfully it would have launched its occupants into the neighbor's yard when placed in the upright position!

"Hey, Ed," I tried to console him before he propelled himself into a deep depression over his fixing failure. "Of the people in this world who could have fixed this chair, how many would be able to stand up in front of a large, diverse audience and bring the book of Hebrews to life, making it

applicable to everyone in the room? In my opinion, that's much finer than being a fixer!"

He didn't reply, but he did kind of smile.

My prayer for today:

You have gifted all of us in different ways, Lord. While some teach, others work in administration. While some serve, others encourage. While some lead, others are needed to follow. While some make beautiful music, others (with absolutely no musical ability) write books. Help me enjoy the gifts You have given me and celebrate the talents of others. Don't let me hamper Your plans or question Your appointments by allowing myself to feel either jealous or superior. Give me a *contributing* heart today, dear God, one that looks for ways to use the gifts You have given me to help others in their walk with You.

Amen.

Gigging Gar and Grappling Gators

Wisdom is a shelter as money is a shelter, but the advantage of knowledge is this: that wisdom preserves the life of its possessor.

Ecclesiastes 7:12

What a surprise! I walked into the family room and there were all four of my sons watching television. It wasn't that all four of them were in the same room at the same time that caught my attention. Nor was it the fact that they were all content to be watching the same show without vying for control of the buttons that amazed me. It was that my four

163

sons were engrossed in a show that was airing on the Discovery Channel!

This channel had always been considered anathema by my children, probably because it was often mentioned at school in conjunction with homework assignments and science reports. I had never known them to flip it on of their own accord. But sure enough, closer investigation indicated that they were watching a nature episode filmed in Australia.

"Hey, guys, what are you watching?" I asked in hopes of joining them in a rare moment of self-induced learning.

"SHHH!" they immediately hushed my exuberance. "It's the Crocodile Hunter and he's about to get bitten by a common Brown snake—one of the most poisonous snakes in the whole wide world!"

Sure enough, there was a pudgy-faced, wild-eyed man flat on his belly inching his way backward across the dry, dusty outback desert. A long, brown, stiff-necked snake swayed back and forth about two feet from his face. It was poised and ready to strike. The strange outdoorsman froze as the snake lowered its head. It slithered toward him. The moment was intense. Everyone in the family room held his breath,

including me. The snake crawled right up to the man's sunburned face, brushed its head across his pudgy cheek . . . then crawled away.

We started to breathe again.

"EEOWW!" the man leapt to his feet screaming something like, "Crikey! That was sooo cool. I was just kissed by a Brown, my friend. Have a look at this! I'll tell you what—that's really great for the ratings, mate!" His adrenaline was obviously pumping; his eyes were popping out in excitement; he was about to swallow the camera as he tried desperately to convey the emotions of the moment to anyone who would listen, anyone who was trapped on the opposite side of the lens.

"He is so crazy!" my kids whooped and hollered their approval. "What an idiot!" they exclaimed with obvious, teenage-style adulation. "Mom, this guy actually wrestles crocodiles! He rides wild camels and plays with bird-eating spiders." They proceeded to tell me about his many antics, usually seen on the Animal Planet channel, that have made him a new cult hero for Generation X. "Everyone watches him," they exclaimed.

I wasn't quite as thrilled anymore about my children's new fascination with the Discovery Channel, especially a few days later when I heard tales about one of my own son's latest fishing expeditions. It seems that he and his buddies had been out gigging for gar and fishing for bass and had come across some baby alligators. Feeling the exciting call of the wild that the Crocodile Hunter had so vividly instilled in them, they had leapt into the water, grabbed the gators, and snapped photos of each other holding baby alligators in their arms.

I discovered the pictures.

"It was the best—the absolute wildest fishing trip I ever went on, Mom! It was soooo cool! Besides, everyone else was  doing it, and no one was getting hurt!" He tried to lure me in with his wild-eyed excitement when I demanded an explanation.

"Well, it might be 'great for the ratings, mate,' but it's no way to get your mom to let you go out with your buddies on another fishing expedition. I'll tell you what, my friend, you're grounded! And, by the way, you're not allowed to watch the Discovery Channel anymore!"

I guess knowledge and wisdom don't always equate!

My prayer for today:

Wisdom, Lord, is something I have tried so hard to instill in my children. I have taught them that true wisdom only comes from You, that they should turn to You in every situation. Yet in their youthful exuberance they so often jump in headfirst without ever looking to You for guidance. Yes, their careless and unwise decisions often upset me, but when I look at my own life, I am even more distressed. There are so many times when I am faced with a decision that I do not seek Your guidance or advice. Beginning today, may my children learn by my example how to seek wisdom. Let them observe a praying mother who seeks the counsel of the God she proclaims. Give me a *consistent* heart, dear God, one that practices what it preaches and one that turns to You for knowledge.

Amen.

Missing the Manual

---

*This is what the LORD says—your Redeemer, the
Holy One of Israel: "I am the LORD your God,
who teaches you what is best for you,
who directs you in the way you should go."*

Isaiah 48:17

I have always thought that children should come into
this world with instruction manuals attached to them.
Dishwashers and lawn mowers do. Their manuals not only
list all the parts involved and how to keep them functioning
smoothly, but they tell you what to do when something goes
wrong. There's a technical support number to call for advice
if things get really bad, and, if all else fails, you can just
package up the product and return it to the manufacturer!

Shouldn't kids come with such information and guarantees?

Sure, the pediatrician gives you a list of shots as you leave the hospital. The nurse hands you a pamphlet telling you when to start feeding the infant oatmeal and what to do the first time your child catches a cold or swallows a marble. La Leché even offers a toll-free number for advice, but it deals with only one area of childrearing.

I'm quite aware that the library has all kinds of reference books outlining the developmental stages of life, and I've seen umpteen books explaining exactly how to potty train a strong-willed child. I realize many great books have been written on how to raise emotionally and spiritually healthy children. But what I need is a manual stocked with a few more of the practical facts of childrearing—hard, cold facts on how to get them through the intricacies of everyday life.

I want to be given a list of science fair projects that are guaranteed to take no more than three hours of my time and can still get my child (at least) a "B."

I want a book that will contain practical ideas on how to build a functional family dwelling. It should make suggestions such as: "Houses built for the purpose of raising kids must be constructed with at least one solid cement wall containing no windows or doors. Such a wall will become the focal point for neighborhood play. It is guaranteed to supply hours of free fun without the additional cost of broken windows."

I want to be warned that every neighbor who buys cheese-and-cracker fund-raisers from my kids will expect me to buy wrapping-paper products from theirs. Someone should inform parents that it would be cheaper and smarter to donate twenty bucks to the school up front and avoid the hassle of collecting money and distributing cheese balls that nobody really wants and nobody will ever eat!

I would like to know early on in the child-raising process that simple things like flashlights and measuring tapes can fascinate kids for hours, and that a hammer and nails will get a lot more use than an expensive video game.

I would like to know what the phone-calling rules are. Is it really okay for girls to call boys these days? If so, does that

just include homework calls, or is it acceptable for the girls to arrange for dates and ask boys to the prom?

I would also like some pointers on how to keep my cool when my fifteen-year-old son announces that he is going to the big city on Friday night with his buddies, and I find out that the guy who will be driving just passed his driver's exam—the day before.

Yes, I think *The Complete Book on Raising Kids* would come in very handy. Unfortunately, most of us would probably ignore such an instruction manual (just like we ignored the one that came with the bicycle), until we messed things up so badly they couldn't be salvaged.

Others might study the manual too deeply, accepting it as the ultimate authority in childrearing. They wouldn't feel the need to turn to God with a trustful heart and a faithful smile.

I guess being stuck raising kids without a complete how-to manual is a rather compelling way for God to get us to depend on Him!

My prayer for today:

Lord, there is so much wisdom waiting for me in the Scripture—knowledge that You have placed there to help me through every situation in life. Yet, seldom do I take the time to look for it. I tend to trust my own instincts, the advice of a friend, or the norm of the culture without ever seeking Your advice or reading Your instructions. Help me spend special time in Your Word today learning what You want me to know. Please show me (and my children through me) the right way to face each new situation. Give me a *learning* heart, dear God, one that seeks instruction from You.

Amen.

Ode to
Jonathan A.

*Be happy, young man, while you are young, and let
your heart give you joy in the days of your youth.*

Ecclesiastes 11:9

I offered to take you to Bobby's house,

But you didn't want to go.

"Steven's house is 'funner,'

But his basketball net's too low."

You don't want to roller skate

Or walk down by the lake.

You're sick of playing Sega,

And you're tired of your snake.

You're starving like a lion,

But there's nothing good to eat.

Apples make your teeth hurt;

Chocolate cake is way too sweet.

You hate the freckles on your nose

And wish your legs would grow.

You're sick of sunny weather—

Want to play out in the snow.

I should let you "slob out"

And sleep with hair that's wet,

Because . . . well, lots of reasons,

Which at the moment you forget.

Your pogo stick is rusty,

Your kite's up in a tree.

Forget about the train set—

It's been broken since age three.

You don't have any money,
So you can't go to the store
Even for some baseball cards—
Which you aren't collecting anymore.

You don't like geography
Can't find Asia on the map.
Ain't learnin' much in English
And in science class you nap.

You'd like to beat up Megan
(Last week you even offered),
Cause you don't want any love notes
Unless they come from Cindy Crawford.

Nothing's worth the effort,
And nothing's fun to play.
You're much too old to throw a fit
Still too young to move away.

You might have fun at Disney
If you could go all by yourself.

(Pardon me for asking, but . . .
Could it be that you are twelve?)

My prayer for today:

Lord, help me to be able to smile as my children go through the various emotions and stages of growing up. You have blessed me with wonderful children, but there are times I can't understand what's going on inside their hearts and minds—especially when they choose not to talk to me and share their problems or pains. During these times, keep me especially faithful in my prayers for them. When they speak may I be a great listener and not always feel the need to advise or correct. Please show me some special ways to communicate my love to them today. Give me an *understanding* heart, dear God, one that brings happiness to the hearts of the children You have placed in my life.

Amen.

Someone Else's Kids?

*Like arrows in the hands of a warrior are sons
born in one's youth. Blessed is the man
whose quiver is full of them.*

Psalm 127:4-5

We've been thinking about calling the producers of the television show "Unsolved Mysteries." Perhaps an in-depth probe by Diane Sawyer would produce better results. Maybe a show dealing with UFO encounters would actually be more appropriate.

Whatever, or whoever—we need help! We would like to determine the true genetic origins of our children. The four we are raising most certainly could not have come from our loins.

First of all, they all like country music, something which we, as parents, think is an abomination and a desecration of true music. For some reason, however, its woeful tunes strike a chord somewhere deep within their souls. They listen to it for hours.

They also drool over every truck that revs a 350 engine or looks like it belongs in the back pasture of some rundown farm. One of our supposed sons has gone so far as to buy a 1976 Chevy pickup with forty-inch tires! He's in great shape if there's ever a major flood in the area. However, he gets soaked every time there's a minor rain. The windows don't close properly, and one of the doors leaks like a sieve. There's no air conditioner, and the heater was disconnected when the CD player was installed. It guzzles gas, and the gauge doesn't work. Consequently, he has to walk many miles alongside the highway carrying a gas container every time he runs out. He doesn't seem to mind one bit—but just try and get him to walk out on the front driveway to get the morning paper!

Each of the kids who call us Mom and Dad is now significantly taller than we are. Ben (the eighteen-year-old, who also owns the truck), is now 6'4" and still growing like a weed. He loves to play basketball, the one sport at which his alleged

Dad, due to gravity restrictions, never excelled. All four of them are very involved in baseball. Not one of them followed the dad they live with into his favorite sport of football.

The children we are raising think that reading is a waste of time. ("If the book's any good, it'll be on video.") They complain that cleaning is useless, since everything gets messy again anyway. They insist that vegetables are better off left in the ground than placed on the dinner table. And they believe that lifting weights at the YMCA is more important than doing yard work at home.

These cannot be our real children! Without a doubt, any children blessed with our genes would love rock and roll music from the '70s. They would be happy to drive an air-conditioned compact car. They would be more our size and enjoy the things we enjoy, including a tidy house and a manicured yard.

Do you suppose it's possible that four different hospitals in four different states, in a matter of less than seven years, messed up and handed out babies to the wrong set of parents—namely us?

I do!

But I have to admit—we're having a ball raising someone else's kids!

My prayer for today:

Thank You, Lord, for the children You have placed in my life—for all the joys and pains, the lessons and love, the emotions and effort that are part of the challenge of raising them to serve You. Help me be as diligent in raising them as a young warrior is in putting his arrows into service. May the targets I direct them toward be pleasing to You, and may I faithfully guide them toward these goals every day. Give me a *persistent* heart, dear God, one that won't give up until my children have achieved all that You have purposed for them.

Amen.

The Key

How can a young man keep his way pure?
By living according to your word.

Psalm 119:9

Last week Jonathan turned sixteen, and we gave him a key. No, it was not the key to a brand new Forerunner or Dodge Ram with big lifters and mud tires, although he would have liked that, too. Instead it was a little fourteen-carat gold key that dangles from a gold chain to be worn around his neck. We have given the same gift to each of our sons when they turned sixteen.

It is a gift that is to be presented to his wife on their wedding night. It is a symbol of the purity he has maintained as he has waited just for her—a promise that his body is hers and hers alone.

The key also symbolizes the fact that we, as parents, are fully aware of the temptations and allures offered so freely by

society. It visualizes the promise that we will continuously pray for each child. It is a tangible sign of our expectations (not just our hopes). It is a constant reminder to each son that he must fully obey God's commandments if he wants to reap the blessings and rewards that God has promised.

Originally the key was meant to be a silent pact between family members, later to be shared with wives. "Just something my parents gave me for my birthday," is the only explanation they needed to offer inquisitive friends. We wanted to save them the possible embarrassment and any harassment that could accompany a detailed explanation to fellow sixteen-year-olds. But that's not quite how it has turned out.

Zach, the oldest and therefore the first to receive his key, blurted out his own explanation the first time he was questioned: "It's a symbol of my virginity." No one dared to question him further at the time. "Cool!" was about the only response he received. But later he had many opportunities to share his faith and his views on sex and abstinence. However, from then on, every kid in the world knew why our sons wore keys around their necks once they turned sixteen.

They have been revered and ridiculed, respected and reviled; but they have always remained proud of their keys. Perhaps the funniest incident related to "the key" took place Zach's first week of college. He attended a large party during freshman orientation. Someone (of the female gender) asked him the significance of the key, wondering if it perhaps signified that he was already attached to a young lady back home.

Once again Zach was bluntly honest. He explained, "No, it's a gift from my parents. It symbolizes my virginity, and I'm going to give it to my wife on my wedding night." The girl's jaw dropped open, and she melted in front of him. "That is the sweetest thing I have ever heard in my whole life!" she exclaimed. She ran to tell all her friends, and soon Zach had a dozen or so girls fawning over him and examining his key. As they left the party, one of Zach's new baseball teammates grabbed him and said, "Diaz, that's the best line I've ever heard! Can I borrow your key?"

The keys have been all over the world (including Hawaii, Zimbabwe, Greece, and even little old Fort Meade). They have been mentioned on the radio and pointed out on TV as

baseball announcers have searched for their own explanation of the charm each of the Diaz boys wears around his neck.

Several keys have been lost over the years. One was buried somewhere on a soccer field following a friendly tussle. (Even a high-powered metal detector could not locate it.) Another lies on the bottom of a murky lake as the result of a water skiing wipeout. Each time a key has been lost, we have been begged for a replacement (and we have been happy to oblige).

Well, as I started to tell you, Jonathan just received his key. (There was no way we could have forgotten to give him one. He's been reminding us for over a year.) So I'm sure we'll be adding more key stories to our collection. We know we're adding one more man to society who understands and is willing to live life God's way.

My prayer for today:

Over and over in the Bible, Lord, You provided Your children with visible symbols of Your power and presence. You asked them to build altars and erect monuments. You

gave them rainbows and reminders. You instituted feasts and festivals. All these were ways of constantly prompting them to look at You and walk in Your ways. Help me follow Your example, using Your teaching techniques to bring the Bible into focus in my children's lives. Show me how I can make Your Word and Your ways real to them. Give me a *creative* heart, dear God, one that assists my children in keeping their lives pure.

Amen.

Tripping over Tongues and Toes

A *man's wisdom gives him patience; it is to his glory to overlook an offense.*

Proverbs 19:11

Several years ago, my then five-year-old son and I were having a rough morning. Everything he wanted to do seemed to fit well within my category of unacceptable behavior, and everything I wanted him to do fit easily into his category of unreasonable demands.

At one point I reminded him that he had to wash his hands before he ate his snack. He decided to debate the issue. After a while I insisted that I was not going to discuss it any

further. If he refused to obey me this time, he would not have a snack at all!

I was in the middle of feeding an infant in a high chair and supervising a toddler with finger paints, which meant that my back was turned to my five-year-old during much of the discussion. Having made my final point, I turned to gauge his response. There he stood in the middle of the kitchen floor sticking his tongue straight out at me!

I was shocked. "Matthew," I commanded in disbelief, "go straight to your room immediately!"

I was devastated! How could this child, who was absolutely wonderful 99 percent of the time, show such utter disrespect for anyone, let alone me—his MOTHER! I was the one who had just made him his very own Superman cape; the one who sometimes put blue food coloring in his ice cream so that it would look like Smurf food; the one who snuck out with him after dark to play flashlight tag! How could he treat me like this? Where had I gone wrong? Somehow I felt that his totally unacceptable behavior had to be my fault.

Sensing my utter dismay, Matthew approached me. "Oh, Mommy," he looked up at me with great, big, saucer-sized,

brown eyes filled with tears, "I wasn't sticking my tongue out at you. I was sticking it out at the wall. You just got in the way!"

Later, when I shared this story with a friend, he cracked up. "You know," he said, "in reality Matthew was probably telling the truth. That day he was sticking his tongue out at everything, and you just happened to be there. I know a lot of grown-ups who do that all the time," he continued. "They walk around sticking their tongues out at the whole world. Sooner or later you end up in the way. You just can't help it. You can't take it personally, or it will devastate you."

That was a revelation for me. I had grown up trying to please people all my life. I had gotten straight A's in high school so my mother would be proud of me. I had lettered in three varsity sports to please my dad. I was always the peacemaker when my friends had disagreements. I tried never to ruffle feathers or hurt anyone's feelings. I even dated guys I had absolutely no interest in, because I didn't want to make them feel bad. I was the consummate "pleaser." I couldn't stand for anyone to be upset with me.

But I had found it exhausting, tiptoeing around trying not to step on toes or get in front of tongues. It was a relief to finally understand that some people have such big feet that

it's impossible to avoid them, and such big tongues that it's hard to stay out of their way.

Some days even the people I love the most are going to be upset with me for no real reason, and that's okay. I've realized that sometimes it's their problem. It doesn't always have to be mine. Everyone is entitled to a bad day once in a while.

My prayer for today:

I don't suppose You've ever had a bad day, Lord (and it's mighty good for us humans that You don't!), but we sure do! Please forgive me when I act like a child and stick my tongue out at everything and everybody that comes across my path. Help me to mature beyond the point where this is my reaction to adversity. Teach me to respond to hardship with dignity and grace. And when others are upset at life and find themselves transferring their feelings to me, help me to understand and be willing to forgive. Give me a *strong* heart, dear God, one that doesn't find itself crumbling under the weight of someone else's displeasure.

Amen.

What's Outside the Window?

The LORD is with me; I will not be afraid.
What can man do to me?

Psalm 118:6

There were some complications with my first pregnancy, so as the second trimester began, I was forced to quit work and take it easy. My husband was in his last semester of seminary in Dallas, Texas, and was also working part-time at a Christian conference center several hours away. It was a long commute. With me no longer able to work, we decided to reverse the commute. We moved to the beautiful East Texas countryside, and Ed commuted into the city for school.

I enjoyed the rest and tranquility of the conference center immensely. Each day I took long walks through grassy meadows, read books down by the lake, swam in the Olympic-sized pool, and prepared our home for the arrival of our baby.

Our home was a mobile one nestled between some oak trees in a very large, beautiful horse pasture. However, what was an absolutely lovely location during the daylight hours, could become very lonely when it grew dark—especially if Ed decided to spend the night in Dallas.

Loneliness turned to concern one day. Just as Ed waved goodbye and drove off down the long lane that led to the nearest country road for one of his two-day trips, I received a prank phone call. The caller informed me that he was aware I would be spending the night alone and suggested that he might pay me a visit.

Needless to say, I double-bolted and barricaded the door that night. I put metal objects on the windowsills, so they would clang if anyone knocked them off trying to break in. I stayed up much later than usual and spent extra time praying for God's presence. I asked Him to send a special angel to protect me.

When I finally did decide to go to bed, I only dozed fitfully, startling at every sound. Finally, sometime around 2:30 in the morning, weariness took over and I fell asleep. I was awakened suddenly by the sound of twigs snapping outside my bedroom window. I lay still, holding my breath as long as I could and hoping that I had been imagining the noise. But it happened again. Leaves rustled, and twigs snapped. Then everything was silent.

I couldn't stand it any longer. I threw off the covers; ran to the window; ripped opened the curtains; and screamed at the intruder at the top of my lungs, hoping to scare him more than he was scaring me.

I jumped back startled. There, standing as still and nonplussed as could be, staring through the window, was . . . a horse! He looked at me in a curious sort of way as if to say, "Hey, lady, what's all the fuss about?"

That was the first time I had ever seen a horse at our end of the pasture. I laughed and apologized for screaming at him and told him I would be delighted if he spent the rest of the night right outside the window protecting me. I don't know what his real name was, but I re-named him Gabriel. I slept much better after that, knowing God had sent me a companion.

Since then, whenever I have a fear, I try to remember to peak at it through the curtains before I scream and yell for help. It's amazing how often I find that it's actually a special gift God has waiting for me outside my window.

My prayer for today:

Lord, You know what's outside every window in my life. I know that You don't want me to be careless or cocky, but You also don't want me to be afraid. When I find myself in scary situations, help me to immediately turn to You for care and confidence. Thank You that so often, the things which frighten me the most turn out to be blessings in disguise. Help me walk through life with the calm assurance of Your presence and the peaceful knowledge of Your protection. Give me a *brave* heart, dear God, one that develops poise and confidence from a close walk with You.

Amen.

The "Hurrier I Go" the "Behinder I Get"

Then, because so many people were coming and
going that they did not even have a chance to eat,
[Jesus] said to them, "Come with me by yourselves
to a quiet place and get some rest."

Mark 6:31

I dashed to the grocery store. I had exactly twenty
minutes to shop for dinner before I had to pick up the
children from school. I rushed down the aisles tossing cans of
baked beans, boxes of macaroni and cheese, and packages of

hot dogs into the cart. I zoomed into the shortest checkout aisle (which, of course, had the slowest checkout girl), helped the bag boy throw the groceries into the sacks, and flew out the door.

I arrived at the school barely in time to pick up the kids. Quickly I delivered child number one to his drum lesson, got child number two home to change clothes, threw the grocery bags on the counter, and deposited aforementioned child number two at the soccer field. I then procured child number one from his drum lesson and deposited number three at his friend's house to work on a school project. I made a mad dash back home to check on child number four, who had been home sick all day (but was well enough to be left alone while I scurried around town) and proceeded to cook dinner in the only half hour available for the rest of the evening.

I was interrupted at least twice by phone solicitations. But as Dad pulled into the driveway (having picked up child number three from his friend's house), it seemed possible that a home-cooked meal (minus the hot dog buns, which I had forgotten in my haste at the grocery store), four sons, and two parents were actually going to converge in harmony and synchrony at the dinner table.

As we sat down to eat, I realized that we were missing a child. I had forgotten to retrieve child number two from the ball field. Oh well. Nice try! Another mad dash; another interrupted meal; another fast-paced evening at the Diaz house!

On my way to the ball field I started to think about the hurried life I live. I thought about how much more relaxed dinners had been when I was growing up. All the fast food, instant meals, and timesaving devices that I own have not provided me with any more free time or relaxation than my mother had. Instead, they have given me access to more activities, saddling me with more responsibilities, and consequently increasing the pace at which I live. And it's all my fault. It's a problem of impatience and greed.

Back in the old days, if my great-great-grandparents missed the stagecoach, they simply headed home and waited for one to come the following month. If my great-grandparents missed the train, they'd just hop aboard the one that chugged into town the following week. And my grandparents often had to wait a day or two to catch the bus out of town. But me—if I miss one section of a revolving door, I go into a tizzy. My life becomes totally disrupted and out of sync!

Sadly, I don't think that this is just my problem. Most Americans appear to be in a hurry. We want our children to learn to read before they can run. We want them to hit a ball off a tee before they can tie their own cleats. We want them to have advanced classes in high school so they can finish college early. We want them to climb the corporate ladder faster and higher than we ever could.

So we rush in and out of grocery stores; we can't stand to wait at the doctor's office; we accelerate when a traffic light turns yellow; we even push and shove at the amusement park to get to the front of the line.

It seems that we are in a hurry to do just about everything in our lives, everything except die, that is. It's as if we are racing in the Indy 500. We use every advantage we can think of to get ahead. We take every shortcut available. We strive with every ounce of energy we can muster to stay out in front, until we see the finish line. Then we slam on the brakes and try desperately to relax and enjoy what little time we have left.

We need to slow our lives down now. We've got to stop letting so many "good" things in life get in the way of what is really best. We need to spend more time with our God,

listening to Him and watching Him work. It's so cliché, but we really should take time to smell the roses that He created for us before it's too late.

(By the way, can I smell your roses? Mine are all dead. I must have backed over them in my hurry to get to the ball field!)

My prayer for today:

Slow me down, Lord, so I at least have enough time to talk to You when I'm not on the run. Show me the things that need to be eliminated from my calendar so I can leave spaces for unexpected pleasures from You. Let me see the interruptions as opportunities—opportunities to spend valuable time with my husband or children; opportunities to get to know You; opportunities to minister to someone else; opportunities that will have eternal significance, not just temporal consequence. Give me a *quiet* heart, dear God, one whose only hurry is to enter Your presence.

Amen.

An Unexpected Excursion

The LORD will keep you from all harm—he will watch over your life; the LORD will watch over your coming and going both now and forevermore.

Psalm 121:7-8

I was in a hurry to get to the elementary school. I had to give my fifth-grade son a message before he hopped on his big, blue bike and headed home for the afternoon. But some elderly little lady who could barely see over the top of her steering wheel took up two lanes of traffic and wouldn't let me into the turning lane, so I was late!

I parked at the curb just in time to see my son's camouflage-colored backpack disappear from the parking lot and head toward the one-way street on the opposite side of the school. Once at the street, he took a sharp right turn.

Right? Why did he turn right? Home is left!

What is going on here? I wondered. *Doesn't he know the unwritten rules? Children are supposed to come straight home after school. If they are more than a few minutes late, parents are to immediately form a search party and start looking for them. This implies that at all times children are obligated to follow exactly the same route to and from school. How else are parents expected to know where to start looking for their missing bodies and their mutilated bikes?*

I jumped into my haphazardly parked vehicle and took off after him. I wound my way through throngs of cars and clumps of children until I was finally headed down the same street. By the time I spotted my son again, he had teamed up with several other children his age and was slowly, very slowly, making his way—somewhere. There was a lot of laughing and talking as the amoebic body of kids oozed its way down the street. As they approached an intersection, the group split. My son and several others headed down a side alley that I had never driven. Up and down driveways they rode, hopping curbs with their bike tires and kicking stones with their dangling feet. They pointed toward tall trees and splashed through gutter-streams of sprinkler runoff. I kept my distance, wanting to learn where such a carefree jaunt could possibly lead.

One by one the children peeled off into various driveways, waving goodbye as they headed to their homes. Finally, only my son was left. He shifted into high gear and, pedaling as fast as his legs could go, he zoomed up and down streets that I didn't even know existed.

Unsuspectingly he led me on a wonderful, circuitous route to our home, arriving at exactly the same time he had every other day that year.

"Hey, Mom. Where you been?" he greeted me as I pulled into the driveway behind him.

"Following you home!" I replied.

"Hey, neat route, isn't it? Best one I've found yet!" he offered nonchalantly. He parked and chained his bike in the garage, so it wouldn't get stolen like the last one had.

I was confused. *What is the role of a mother in our often-dangerous society?* I wondered. I wanted to protect my child, yet how could I rob him of experiences like the one he had just had? I treasure such Christopher Robin-type memories from my childhood days.

Our children are bombarded with too many pre-programmed fantasies. They need more expeditions to never-before-explored territories and excursions with unexpected

surprises. But there weren't any paroled child molesters or gang members stalking Pooh and Piglet in the Hundred Acre Wood.

Guess there are just some things I need to leave in God's hands, I decided. The well-being of my children is one of them. I imagine guardian angels love exciting explorations.

My prayer for today:

Thank You, Lord, for the knowledge that You love my children more deeply than I ever could, and that You promise to protect them. Give me the insight to know when it is necessary to fence them in, balanced with the courage to allow them freedom to explore Your world. Please make their childhood memories sweet. It is a daunting task, in this day and age, to know how to protect without being over-protective; to be carefree without being careless. So I pray for a *discerning* heart, dear God, one that knows what is best for my children. (Meanwhile, would You please keep their guardian angels extra alert? Thanks!)

A Backward Glance

"For I know the plans I have for you," declares the
LORD, *"plans to prosper you and not to harm you,*
plans to give you hope and a future."

Jeremiah 29:11

I wrapped the last of the gifts and headed to the post
office. All my nieces and nephews seemed to be graduating at
once. It was impossible to attend ceremonies in Florida,
Pennsylvania, and Arkansas at the same time—so a book and
a check would have to do.

As I pictured them marching across various stages in
their caps and gowns, I was transported back to that huge
event in my own life. It was an event I had not thought
about in a very long time. At first the memories were fuzzy,

but as I allowed them to play out in my mind, they began to clear up and come into focus.

I remembered hoping I wouldn't be late as I rushed out the door that evening. Then the car ran out of gas right on top of the railroad tracks on my way to the football stadium. My younger brother came to my rescue.

I remembered that my hair, which had spent the bulk of the day in rollers, lay limp and stringy down my back due to high humidity and gale force winds preceding a summer storm.

I remembered arriving just in time to hear our band strike up the first few bars of "Pomp and Circumstance" as I raced to my place in line. The first few bars were all they were able to play as the wind whipped the music right off the stands.

I remembered feeling lonely, very lonely. I was seated with the faculty and dignitaries away from the rest of my friends and fellow graduates. I had been selected to give a speech that night in front of the whole world. The co-valedictorians had been caught drinking on the senior class trip and were graduating in a state of near suspension. They were told that they were lucky to be there at all. They were not allowed to give their speeches. I envied them.

I remembered standing at the podium and thinking how stupid my speech was. I had been advised to go with a "new day, new world" uplifting kind of theme. I was saying things like: "Here we stand on the shores of a new tomorrow . . . sandy beaches spread before us . . . a new day dawning." It was a bright, rosy, challenging speech, but I knew that no one there was feeling particularly bright or rosy or like they needed to face any new challenges.

I didn't say that the beaches we were about to land on were really full of sharp, jagged rocks and steep, treacherous cliffs. But as I looked around, I knew they probably were.

There sat Joey with his head shaved. He had been the captain of our football team. The day before graduation he had enlisted in the army. We all knew that he would be sent to Vietnam.

Behind him sat Mary, my best friend, in her white cap and gown. Her boyfriend had just ditched her, but somewhere

under that gown was his baby. He didn't know it. Nor did her mother.

Vinnie had hobbled in on crutches. He was lucky to be alive after a terrible car accident six weeks before. "He fell asleep at the wheel," his parents explained. But we all knew he had been drinking.

As I plodded through the speech, my mind inventoried the class, and my soul ached. Ironically, just as I finished, a gust of wind caught my manuscript and blew it off the podium, across the field, and into oblivion. I watched helplessly, feeling that somehow justice had been wrought on that useless piece of paper. The speech didn't really belong to me—or to my class. Our idealism had already been shattered by the assassinations of Martin Luther King Jr., John F. Kennedy, and his brother Bobby; by machine-gun fire in the jungles of Vietnam; by loud, angry protests on the very college campuses we were about to attend. What hope did we really have?

As I arrived at the post office, my graduation memories ran out of footage. I began to compare them to life as it is now. My best friend married another man who lovingly helped her raise her son.

The two guys who were caught drinking on the senior class trip are doing just fine; one is a renowned eye surgeon and the other a real estate mogul!

Vinnie healed nicely and raised a large family in a house just down the road from where he grew up.

Joey made it back from Vietnam—well, most of him did. It's been a struggle over the years, but he says he's doing fine now.

And me? I've tripped over a few sharp rocks and scaled a few jagged cliffs myself, but I now know that there usually is a sandy shore on the other side. There really are days that dawn bright and rosy.

I wish I still had that speech. It makes a whole lot more sense now than it did that day! I guess that's because I've chosen to see God at work. (It's a lot easier to do when you look backwards.)

My prayer for today:

Thank You, Lord, for the plans You have for me. Thank You that they have brought me to where I am today. Help me to view each situation as part of a beautiful tapestry that You have designed and are now weaving with my life. Don't let me be discontent or gloomy as I await the fulfillment of Your purposes. Give me an *excited* heart, dear God, one that rejoices in the plans that You have for me.

Amen.

Don't Super-size Your Fries

Death and Destruction are never satisfied,
and neither are the eyes of man.

Proverbs 27:20

There is a fast food joint just a few blocks from my house. It's on the way to just about everywhere I need to go. I try to avoid driving past it, treating it as if it dispensed the plague. The problem isn't the roast beef sandwiches that it's famous for or the creamy smooth milk shakes or the service. The problem is the fries. I'm addicted to them. They are the most wonderfully seasoned, curly French fries I have ever tasted. If I drive by slowly and get even the slightest whiff, I can't help myself. I yank the steering wheel, turn into the parking lot, drive up to the window and order some "to go." Then I hate myself for a week.

Well, the other day I was thirsty—very thirsty, and I was on my way to a three-hour stint at the ball field to watch my sons play baseball. As I drove past the wicked joint, I decided to pull in—but not for fries! No, I was absolutely, positively not going to get any fries. I just wanted a drink.

Sure enough, as the window opened, out wafted that smell. Once again, it was too enticing for me to refuse. I had to have some of those wonderfully seasoned, curly French fries! I hadn't had lunch, and I was kind of hungry; so it was justifiable, right? I decided I might as well go ahead and order a sandwich to go with them, since they come in combo packages for not much more than the price of the fries and drink.

After I placed my order, the smiling cashier (who I later realized was actually smirking) asked me if I would like to super-size my order. It would only cost me a few more cents.

Why not?

So super-size it I did!

Along with a cup of soda that could quench a camel's thirst, she handed me the largest box of curly fries I had ever seen. I was in hog heaven.

I scarfed down a few. Oh, they were so good! Between bites of my sandwich, I kept stuffing my mouth with fries. Long after the sandwich was on its way through my digestive system, the box of fries was still brimming. I ate and ate and ate. I was getting full. Very full. Yet I kept feeding my face. I couldn't let those wonderfully seasoned, curly French fries go to waste, could I?

My drink had long since been reduced to ice chips, but there was still a half a box of fries, which I slowly kept munching. Soon I was bloated with fries. I felt like they were sticking out of my ears. As I swallowed the last fry I began to feel sick.

I sat through a whole ball game holding my stomach and hating those curly French fries. I never wanted to see another one as long as I lived.

The second the ball game was over, the kids came running over to me. "Can we head over to the big stadium? The Tigers are playing a doubleheader!" they inquired, bursting with enthusiasm.

"No gang, not now. I think we've had just the right amount of baseball for one day," I groaned from my crunched

position. "Let's not super-size baseball. Super-sizing ruins too many good things."

They looked at me as if I had been out in the sun much too long.

"Well, then can we at least stop and get some curly fries on the way home?"

"Ohhhhhh!" All I could do was groan.

My prayer for today:

Lord, teach me about satisfaction in all areas of my life. When I look at my calendar or glance around my house, I realize that so much of what I do, and most of what I have, is based on overindulgence. Help my life shine in its simplicity. In a world that is often very complicated and self-gratifying, help me learn to be content without being full. Help me learn to be satisfied without "having it all." Somehow help me be able to convey to my children the freedom found in simple things and the joy found in satisfaction. Give me a *satisfied* heart, dear God.

Amen.

The Secret of Silence

The quiet words of the wise are more to be heeded than the shouts of a ruler of fools.

Ecclesiastes 9:17

"Good game, Ben!"

It was a simple, motherly comment following a game in which my son's junior high school baseball team had routed their opponents by ten runs. It was an honest, sincere statement; but, unbeknownst to me, it was loaded with gunpowder. When it hit Ben's ears it exploded!

"GOOD! Did you say 'GOOD'? Paahhh!" Hot air burst out of his mouth (along with a little saliva).

"Ben, you did a great job catching!" I reacted, trying to defend my honest comment and his baseball abilities. After

all, he had crouched behind home plate for the better part of two hours on a hot, humid afternoon wearing about twenty pounds of catcher's gear, and very few balls had even come close to getting past him.

"You obviously didn't see my throw to third when their guy was stealing," he snarled. "I should have had him by a mile! But no! What did I do? I launched the ball clear into left field!"

"Hey, the batter got in your way. There was no way you could have gotten off a clean throw." I continued attempting to justify my viewpoint and build him up at the same time. "Besides, the guy didn't even end up scoring."

"I stunk it up, Mom! Quit trying to make me into some kind of hero."

I thought about the sky-high foul pop-up he had dived for and caught to end an inning and the wild pitch he had leapt after in order to save the pitcher's ERA. I had a lot more valid arguments I could make, but I was starting to get a little ticked at the way he was treating me. After all, I had just spent my whole afternoon watching a boring junior high baseball game. I could think of lots of things that would have been more enjoyable than sitting on hot metal bleachers for two hours shading my eyes from the sun. His attitude obviously needed a little work.

I was about to let him have it, but for some reason I decided to keep my mouth shut.

Silently he packed up his gear and loaded it into the car. Silently we drove home. Silently he showered while I made him a sandwich. Silently he plopped himself down across the table from me and began to scarf down his food.

For a second my eyes caught his. "I love you," was all that I could think to say. So I said it.

There was silence for about two minutes, then . . .

"I think I flunked my science test today!" he blurted out. He stared at me, totally challenging my assertion of love and ready to attack any response I might make.

So that's what's bugging him, I thought. Again, a million responses went though my brain, things like: *Well, you knew for a week that you were going to have that test. You should have studied more. Or Maybe you should cut out the baseball and hit*

the books a little harder, young man. Or Gee, Ben! I spent two whole hours going over that stuff with you last night! What's so tough about the circulatory system anyway? (For some reason Ben was having a tough time getting into body parts and their functions.)

But looking at him I knew that nothing I could say would do much good. So I just replied, "Like I said, I love you."

He shook his head at me (obviously, he thought I was nuts) and got up to unlock the front door for his two older brothers who were just arriving home from a late high school game.

"Hey, how'd ya do, Benny?" they asked as they burst through the door with all their baseball gear.

"Great!" he replied. "You should have seen the foul pop-up I snagged. You'd never have gotten near it!" he ribbed his older brother, Matt, who is also a catcher.

"Hey, can you help with some extra credit for my science class?" he turned to Zach (who has always been good at body parts).

I just shook my head in silence and made more sandwiches.

My prayer for today:

Lord, I am just beginning to understand the power and importance of my tongue. With it I can convey my needs, my knowledge, my personality, and so much more. Teach me to use my tongue only to heal, never to hurt. Help me to use it quietly, to accomplish positive things for You. As I both nurture and admonish my children, I want to maintain my tongue with godly composure and quiet tranquillity. Please give me a *quiet* heart, God, one that will allow only gentle words to come out of my mouth.

Amen.

An Unscheduled Appointment

Many are the plans in a man's heart,
but it is the LORD'S purpose that prevails.

Proverbs 19:21

I don't remember exactly where I was headed that day. I do recall that it had just finished raining, that I was all dressed up, and that once again I was in a big hurry. I wheeled around a corner and slammed on my brakes. As I brought my fishtailing van under control, I realized that I was stuck behind a long line of slow-moving vehicles.

I glanced quickly ahead to assess the problem. About a block away, spreading itself across the lawns of several large

homes, was a seething, pulsating mob of teenagers. It was growing by the second. It was immediately apparent that some type of intense altercation was already underway.

Not one of the cars in front of me stopped. Nor did any of the vehicles headed in the opposite direction. The drivers and passengers just gawked and drove slowly by. No one seemed to want to get involved, but everyone seemed to want to catch a glimpse of the action.

Something that seemed to come from somewhere deep inside my chest compelled me to pull up onto the sidewalk and stop. Without very much thought (even a modicum of brainwork would probably have turned me into another rubbernecking passerby), I stepped out of my vehicle; and in my high heels and dressy dress I approached the riotous mob on the muddy lawn.

The crowd slowly parted as I walked toward its center. Everyone stared at me as if I were a ghost, and for some reason, they stepped aside to let me pass. In the center of the fray, I was shocked to find two young, teenage girls beating each other with a vengeance. There was blood and hair

everywhere. They were sparing no effort or ounce of energy as they ripped and punched and pulled and kicked.

I stepped closer and put one hand on each of their flailing shoulders. Immediately they stopped thrashing and both of them stared at the strange (very stupid), over-dressed lady who was intruding in their affairs.

"It's finished," I said in a low, calm voice. "Your fight is over, and you can both go home now."

They squinted their eyes and scowled at me. I stepped between them just in case they didn't wish to comply.

Facing the obvious aggressor, I cupped her face in my hands. Two very angry, very beautiful eyes flashed at me, but she didn't move.

"You are a beautiful young lady," I said softly. "God did a gorgeous job when He created you."

Huge tears filled her eyes, and her whole body softened for just a few seconds. She quickly regrouped, picked up her belongings, gathered a few friends, and mumbled something about "getting out of here before the cops show up."

"Who was that? What did she say?" her friends inquired as they left the scene.

"I don't know," and "Nuthin'," she replied. Then she turned around and smiled at me.

I winked and then blinked as I was forced to fight back my own tears.

I patched up the other girl and gave her a big hug and told her how special she was. She thanked me and even hugged me back.

Everyone seemed to evaporate into the landscape. There I stood in the middle of an empty lawn with mud on my shoes and blood on my dress.

There was no way I was going to make it to my appointment on time, but it just didn't matter. This unplanned interruption took precedence over my previously scheduled appointment—whatever it was!

My Prayer for today:

Lord, I have many plans and purposes for my life. They cause me to hustle my way through each day not leaving

much room for change. Help me approach each interruption as a God-ordained appointment rather than a nuisance. Please feel free to redirect me and refocus my attention today. Give me a *flexible* heart, dear God, one that is happy to be interrupted by You.

Amen.

A Sacrifice for the Sake of the Kids

If a man is lazy, the rafters sag; if his hands are idle, the house leaks.

Ecclesiastes 10:18

Just in case you visit my house this summer and notice that it needs cleaning, please let me explain. It's not because I'm lazy that there is a thin layer of dust on every flat surface. And it's not because I'm a slob that my wooden furniture has taken on a strange, grayish hue. It's because I have made an intellectual, rational—maybe even sacrificial—decision: I have decided to quit dusting for the sake of my children.

Have you noticed that many more children are diagnosed with allergies these days than ever before? This is not just because there are more allergists around who need to support their families (although that may be a contributing factor). Nor is it due to a change in our ecosystem. Rather, I think we parents are to blame. We have succumbed to the notion that our children must be raised in relatively dust-free environments.

Think about it.

In the "olden days," children had to walk many miles down long, dusty roads to get to school. They worked many hours out of doors on hot, dusty farms. They played baseball on dusty, wind-swept sandlots. They lived in houses with open windows and slept on dusty, straw-filled mattresses. Their bodies were used to dust, and consequently grew accustomed to handling its negative effects. Did these children take allergy shots every two weeks at the local clinic? I think not!

Our children, on the other hand, ride the two blocks to school in air-conditioned cars or on tightly sealed buses. They

travel along paved roads, which are sometimes even cleaned by city-operated street sweepers.

Our children seldom work before the age of sixteen, and when they do, it is usually inside an air-conditioned mall. They play baseball on neatly manicured grass with hard-packed clay. They sleep on hypoallergenic mattresses in air-conditioned rooms.

Consequently, children today are prone to sneeze every time a dust mite is hatched inside the sleeper sofa on the far side of the family room.

So using the same principles by which the allergists operate and seem to profit greatly (my son's allergist just returned from a fishing trip that took him to every exotic island ever mentioned in a Beach Boys album!), I am boycotting dusting. By not dusting, I am allowing my children to be exposed to a gradual increase in the level of dust in my home. They are thereby receiving a natural inoculation to the dust mite and will over time be desensitized to any potential allergy-evoking effects.

I have also realized that there are several side benefits to non-dusting. A dusty coffee table can provide a tremendous tactile surface on which young children can practice their alphabet and increase their small motor skills. Dust eradicates the need for messy items such as finger paints, and it's a whole lot cheaper than purchasing an Etch-A-Sketch.

For teenagers, phone numbers and messages can easily be jotted down on a dusty end table when no pen or paper is available. Also, I'm checking into the possibility that a layer of dust on a television screen can actually provide an absorbent barrier to harmful radiation, thus reducing damage to delicate brain cells.

I'm sure you can now understand why, purely as a sacrifice for my children, I haven't dusted the furniture all summer. I don't look at this as a lazy excuse. I'd rather think of it as a valuable experiment.

A-a-a-a-a-choooooooo! Can anyone find the box of tissues? I left it somewhere on the coffee table. It must be camouflaged under a layer of dust!

My prayer for today:

Lord, I have to admit that the mundane monotony of tasks such as vacuuming and dusting, doing laundry, and making dinner every day sometimes drives me crazy. Help me find fresh ways to approach my duties, and please instill in me a happy new attitude to coincide. Help my children to develop healthy work habits from observing and imitating mine. Give me a *refreshed* heart, dear God, one that wants to tackle each chore with vim and vigor.

Amen.

Another Chunk of Cheetah Chow

---

*Buy the truth and do not sell it; get
wisdom, discipline and understanding.*

Proverbs 23:23

We watched a National Geographic special the other day
on the Learning Channel. It was all about the animals of the
African plains. We saw lions and cheetahs and hyenas as they
stalked, captured, devoured, and digested their prey. It was
truly an educational experience. I learned far more than I
ever wanted to know about survival on the Serengeti.

In one particular sequence, we observed several cheetahs
in pursuit of a water buffalo entrée for their evening meal.

Three or four cheetahs charged in and disrupted an entire herd of the wallowing beasts. Then one cheetah took off after a predetermined buffalo, which had unwisely separated itself from the crowd. It was interesting to note that the cheetah did not target a big, daddy buffalo who was also off on its own, or even a little bitty calf nearby. It was a nice, well-rounded, somewhat slow mama that was selected for dinner that day.

The buffalo stopped, turned around, and held the cheetah, who was immediately joined by his preying partners, at bay for several minutes. She warded off all attacks and attackers with long slashing sweeps of her huge horns. She was doing just fine. She could have stayed there swinging her head all day until her attackers grew weary of the stalemate. But for some unwise reason, she decided to dash (in a lumbering sort of way) for freedom.

Dumb move!

Soon she was exhausted and found herself trapped between some rocks and a panting pack of cheetahs. In a matter of minutes, she was a goner—nothing more than

another piece of meat in the universal game of self-preservation and survival of the fittest! The cheetahs snapped and snarled over her carcass. It was sad, but that mother water buffalo was a victim of her own unwise decisions and her lack of discipline. Both were sure setups for failure. It was too late for her to learn from the experience.

A few days later my sons decided to put what they had learned on that television program into practice. Their old video game had bitten the dust a few weeks before, and somehow they had each been able to scrape together about $30 of their own, hard-earned cash to buy a new one. They knew that we, their parents, would feel that this was a silly  waste of $120, that they should save their money for more important things like a college education or new underwear. They knew that we would make wise objections like, "We don't care if everyone else on the planet has one. We're not everyone else's parents." So they resorted to the innate techniques that lie hidden in the depths of all living beings. They began *the hunt*. No, they didn't go after the big, daddy water buffalo. Just like the cheetahs, they went after the somewhat slower, much more vulnerable mama. And just like the cheetahs, they separated their prey from the safety of the herd.

That Saturday, while their father was out of town teaching a weekend seminar, they informed me that they would like to accompany me to the mall. It was an unusual request, and I was rather wary. When I confronted them for an explanation of their new fascination with the mall, they acknowledged their plan. I swayed my head back and forth explaining how this was not how I wanted them to waste their wad of money.

For several minutes, I held them at bay. If I had stood my ground for just a few more minutes they probably would have grown weary. However, as they circled me mercilessly, whining and reasoning, begging and cajoling, and even offering to help out extra around the house for the next twenty years, I made an unwise, undisciplined decision! In a final fit of frustration and feeling helplessly vulnerable, I gave in and drove them to the mall—just to check out the prices.

Dumb move!

There I was, trapped between a store clerk and a panting pack of kids—and you know the rest of the story. I was a

goner . . . just another chunk of cheetah chow in the universal game of self-preservation and survival of the fittest.

The kids snipped and snarled all the way home over who would play the first game, while I slowly but surely realized that I had become a victim of my own unwise decisions and lack of discipline. Hopefully it isn't too late to gain a little understanding and wisdom for the next go 'round—an opportunity the mama water buffalo never received!

My prayer for today:

Lord, as I strive to bring up my children in ways that are right and pleasing to You, I know that I am often going to make unwise decisions. Help me learn from my mistakes early in the adventure so that later, when consequences are greater and much more is at stake, wisdom will rule over weariness; discipline will conquer despair; and understanding will undergird each decision I make. Give me a *strong* heart today, dear God, one that won't grow weary in accomplishing Your work and Your will for my children.

Amen.

A Little out of Sync

There is a time for everything, and a season for every activity under heaven.

Ecclesiastes 3:1

Do you have any idea how hard it is to get the streaks off a window that has been thoroughly sprayed and scrubbed with hair spray?

Months after my then four-year-old son decided to help me with my chores, I found myself cleaning my front windows every time the setting sun sent its slanting rays through the glistening, smeary mess. No amount of suds or elbow grease could eradicate the greasy smudges.

"I cleaned the windows real good for you!" he boasted proudly as he displayed his workmanship. "I growed real big, so I cleaned up real high!"

Yep, he sure had!

"Thank you," I managed to utter through tight lips and clenched teeth. "You are so sweet. But I think you should let Mommy clean the windows from now on. When you're even bigger and can reach all the way to the top, you can clean them whenever you want to!"

Then there was the time that two of my sons joined forces with a neighborhood friend to clean his grandma's new car.

"It was muddy, so we squirted all the mud off!" they proudly announced.

And they sure had! Only now the mud was all on the *inside*! In their youthful exuberance, they had forgotten to roll up the windows.

"From now on you have to ask us before you turn on the hose," we legislated. "When you're big enough to ride your own bicycles to school, then you will be big enough to wash the car every Saturday," we promised in our own eager anticipation of such a day.

There was also a time in their lives when my four sons would beg me every week from early spring until late fall to allow them to weed the flower beds. "We're big boys now. We

know which ones are weeds," they would insist as they ardently uprooted my newly planted marigolds.

"By the time you're old enough to play soccer and hit a baseball, you can help in the yard every week," we reasoned, trying to supply them with a tangible timeline.

Well, three of our four sons are now well over six feet tall, and the other is not far behind. They can touch the ceiling (and their hand prints prove it), not to mention the top of the windows. They ditched their bicycles long ago and three of the four have their driver's licenses. (The fourth is a terror on a golf cart!)

All of them have long since graduated from soccer and can even hit a curve ball. So the windows are clean, the cars are washed, and the flower beds are weedless. Right?

Wrong!

Not one of my sons has been seen trying to clean a window since the hair spray day so many years ago. Not a hose has been aimed toward a dirty car, and not a weed has been pulled (or even a marigold!) without much coercion and consternation. Somehow the timing seems to be a little out of sync in such areas of life. Desire and ability never seem

to quite coordinate with each other. Just ask my eighty-six-year-old Mom. She'd love to be able to wash the car and weed her own garden again!

My prayer for today:

There are definitely facets and phases of life that I don't understand, Lord. For instance, I can't figure out why You endowed two-year-olds with more energy than You allotted to their mothers. (In my humble opinion, it should be the other way around!) But I am learning that it is not my job to figure You out. You only ask that I trust You and choose satisfaction over discontentment, acceptance over dissent, and determination over despair. You are the absolute, sovereign God of the universe, and You love me. That is all I really need to know. Give me an *embracing* heart, dear God, one that eagerly accepts what You have chosen for me during this time of my life.

Amen.

A Caring Kind of Shampoo?

Look to my right and see; no one is concerned for me. I have no refuge; no one cares for my life. I cry to you, O LORD; I say, "You are my refuge, my portion in the land of the living."

Psalm 142:4-5

It started out as a dismal Saturday in every way. First the car wouldn't start, so I couldn't get to the grocery store for milk. Then the dog escaped from the back porch and ran out into the rain. I was the only one awake to go after him. To top it all off, while I was out chasing him through the neighbor's rose garden and splashing through the street gutters, the kids woke up, and one of them had the audacity to eat the last Pop Tart—which was the only thing that could have possibly salvaged the beginning of my day.

To make matters even worse, when I tried to share my woes with my children, they were far too interested in reading their cereal boxes and watching Saturday morning cartoons to care that I was sopping wet and extremely perturbed. (My husband was off on another business trip!) I stomped upstairs to get a shower in an attempt to restart my day.

It was then that I discovered the truth about my shampoo. Out of some extreme need for camaraderie or companionship, I began to read the label on the almost-empty bottle. To my surprise, I found that this product, which I had unwittingly taken for granted ever since I purchased it several weeks before, "truly cares about the needs of my hair!" It notices every strand and is designed to make each one of them "reach its fullest potential." Wow!

My kids on the other hand, probably wouldn't notice if I shaved all my hair off! Oh, they might make some comment like, "What's gotten into Mom today?" But that would be about the extent of it. I can't think of a single strand of my hair that matters very much to them at all—except for a few gray ones they like to tease me about.

I kept reading and discovered that my shampoo "works hard for me, building up each strand of hair from the follicle, causing it to bounce and shine." My kids have never worked

hard for me a day in their lives! And when they are forced to do their chores, nothing seems to be left shiny. Everything is just kind of stuffed into a corner and vacuumed around.

What's more, I found that my shampoo knows exactly when to quit! It "knows precisely how much to condition each strand of hair so that not one of them is left limp and lifeless by over-conditioning." My kids don't have a clue when to quit. They can keep a discussion about whose turn it is to feed the dog going for close to two hours while the dog lies limp and lifeless in the back yard.

On top of everything else, my shampoo is the product of a "unique, technological breakthrough designed specifically to meet the needs of *my* hair!" Besides being caring, compassionate, and conscientious, it is made from all natural products containing everything I will ever need to keep my hair "lustrous and lively!"

My kids are full of unnatural chemicals that come from a diet of fast food burritos, French fries, and soda. No wonder they're such couch potatoes. There is absolutely nothing lustrous or lively about them on a rainy Saturday morning!

I couldn't believe that I had been so oblivious to the intelligence and beauty trapped within the plastic bottle that

I so nonchalantly retrieve from the corner of the shower stall every morning. I purposed to treat my shampoo with a little more respect from that moment on. I contemplated getting rid of the kids and filling the house with smart, conscientious, caring shampoo.

I was feeling a little better about myself as I bounced back downstairs following a rather lengthy, albeit very educational shower. I decided to give the kids one more shot.

"Hey, kids! Does anyone want to go to the mall with me?" I queried.

No reply.

"How about if we stop and get some ice cream on the way home?"

Still no response.

"Hey, we could go visit Uncle Rick and take a tour of his new motor home?"

Nada. They didn't even ask me to quit bugging them. They didn't acknowledge my existence in any way. They were absorbed in a video game.

I turned around, walked upstairs, and headed back to the shower.

Only one problem—I was out of shampoo!

My prayer for today:

There are days, Lord, when I am so overbooked and in demand that I wish everyone would go away and leave me alone. Then there are days, even in the midst of all the turmoil, that I feel so alone, so unwanted and unnecessary, that my heart aches for companionship. Help me remember that You are always there. Nothing can get in the way of Your love for me—a love that is so intimate it knows every detail of every hair on my head! Give me a *comforted* heart, dear God, one that doesn't count on other people (or things) for fulfillment—only on You.

Amen.

Missing the Main Ingredient

Woe to you, teachers of the law and Pharisees, you hypocrites! You give a tenth of your spices—mint, dill and cummin. But you have neglected the more important matters of the law—justice, mercy and faithfulness. You should have practiced the latter, without neglecting the former.

Matthew 23:23

I realized that the boys had made a valiant effort to clean up the syrupy ice cream mess that had landed on the kitchen floor the night before. But once again it had become my job to remove the remaining sticky residue the following

morning. It seemed like all my life I had been cleaning kitchen floors. It had been my usual job every Saturday morning growing up—a consequence of being the only daughter in a family with three children.

But as I mopped, I couldn't help but recall one particular Saturday morning many years before. That day, I had already cleared all the breakfast and lunch dishes off the table. I had wiped the gray, marble-looking countertop, and I had even used a toothpick to clean out the dirt that imbedded itself under the metal strip that ran around its edge. I dusted off the plastic-bottomed chairs and rearranged the calendar that covered a rip in the rooster-and-coffeepot-decorated wallpaper. Then I scrubbed the linoleum floor.

It was a special Saturday. One of my friends from junior high school was coming over to spend the afternoon. Guests didn't show up very often at our ramshackle little house way out in the country (except for the critter kind). Since returning to the United States from Africa, money had been hard to come by for our family. We made do as best we could, but there usually wasn't much left over to share with company.

Mary, however, was a special friend. Well, at least I wanted her to be. She was one of the most popular kids in school. We had been assigned a school project to work on together, and she wanted to see where I lived. (She lived in town where all the rich kids lived.) I really wanted to impress her.

To make her visit more memorable, I had scrounged together enough money to buy the ingredients to make banana splits. I had even bought pre-chopped nuts! Such a special treat would not only provide a welcome study break, but it should also make a great impression on my new friend.

Mary arrived early in the afternoon. After showing her my tiny bedroom (which I had also cleaned immaculately) and telling my nosy brothers to scram, we sat down at the table to do our homework. As I recall, Mary did most of the work. All I could think about was the upcoming banana split break. I hadn't shared with her what I had planned. I wanted it to be a surprise.

About two hours into our project, Mary heaved a weary sigh signaling the perfect time.

"Hey, how about we make some banana splits?" I asked nonchalantly as if I was used to making them three or four times a day.

"Wow! That would be really cool!" Mary was obviously impressed with my plan. I began dragging the bowls and spoons and bananas and whipped cream and caramel and chocolate sauce and nuts and cherries out onto the counter. I peeled two bananas and split them in half lengthwise, placing them in the bowls. Then I started piling the condiments on top.

My creations looked delicious. I noticed that Mary had a kind of weird look on her face, but I surmised that it was probably just from the anticipation of such a special treat. I handed her a spoon and told her to dig in.

We both ate our banana splits in silence. Something was definitely wrong. Although I had only eaten one banana split in my life, I knew that my creation didn't taste like a banana split was supposed to taste. Something seemed to be missing. I couldn't figure out what was wrong, but I chose not to say anything, just in case Mary's tasted fine.

She thanked me, and we went back to work on our project.

On Monday, I was greeted at school by several snickering friends. "So they make banana splits without ice cream where you come from," they teased me.

That was it—the ice cream! I had forgotten the ice cream! In all my efforts to influence and impress my new friend by making banana splits, I had left out the main ingredient! No wonder they tasted so weird! I was humiliated.

I would like to say that I learned a great lesson from my junior high school experience, but I'm afraid that even today I often forget the ice cream. No, I'm not talking about making banana splits. I've got those down now. I'm talking about all the times I forget the most important ingredients in life—like when I focus on my kids' mess-ups rather than their efforts or when I get upset at the stack of dirty dishes by my husband's recliner rather than being thankful that he's a good man who loves God and cares for his family.

You know, the rest of life is just a syrupy goo when you leave out what's really important!

My prayer for today:

Lord, help me not to inadvertently leave out the main ingredient in my life today. As I hustle my way through the busyness, don't let me lose my focus on You. Sometimes I become so intent on impressing others that I find myself concentrating on all the superfluous elements of life and ignoring what is really important—the priority of sharing Your love. Give me the proper focus today, one that will love and lead my children, my husband, and my friends into a closer relationship with You. Give me a *concentrated* heart, dear God, one that is fixed on You.

Amen.

I Raised an Angel and a Devil

---

*All hard works brings a profit, but mere talk
leads only to poverty.*

Proverbs 14:23

I was trudging through a department store with several
toddlers in tow when I spotted a big, red, plastic bat with a
huge, white wiffle ball attached. I recognized immediately
that this combination could provide hours of backyard
pleasure and become the perfect pastime to fill long summer
afternoons. The fact that it was only $2.99 cinched the
decision. I bought it.

As soon as I pulled into the driveway, all my little boys jumped out of the car, grabbed their new paraphernalia, and headed for the backyard. Immediately they started staking out the bases. They displayed an incredible depth of knowledge about a game that I had never even known them to observe. Picnic benches were moved and boundaries were established. The orange tree was foul, the birdbath was fair, and a home run had to sail over the clothesline. And the game began.

Before long, base paths had carved themselves into the backyard grass. I spent endless hours pitching to eager batters and reminding youngsters which way to run the bases. One afternoon I found myself staring at the clouds after being bashed in the head by a hard hit wiffle ball. It was our first indication that Matthew might one day be a slugger. And Zach, who soon convinced us that he was a lefty, began striking me out with two well-placed fast balls and a funky curve.

Once the boys had mastered all the backyard basics I had to offer, Dad was incorporated into the process. Over the ensuing years he taught each one how to stand in the batter's

box, grip a change-up, and take a secondary lead off first base.
He spent endless hours hitting fungos, evaluating curve balls,
raking clay, and driving van loads of high school boys to far-
away fields.

No matter how much we gave them, the boys always
wanted more baseball. They quickly chose to swap wiffle ball
games in the backyard for Saturday t-ball tournaments at the
city field with their buddies. They begged us to sign them up
for Little League teams when their friends did and wouldn't
think of missing a single practice. They invited classmates
over to watch the "Cubbies" on TV and celebrated birthdays
with their teammates at Marchant Stadium.

I realized that baseball had become an obsession when we
spent an entire three-week family vacation visiting all the
major league ballparks within driving distance. The guys can
tell you all about the teams that played on those fields,
pointing out the highest paid hitters and the wiliest pitchers.
I, on the other hand, can tell you where to get the best
bratwurst (Milwaukee); which team has the best organist
(Chicago White Sox); and where not to use the restrooms
(Boston—not one toilet would flush the day we visited
Fenway).

As they entered their high school years, my sons began spending early mornings in the weight room and late afternoons running long distances around the lake. (It was at this point that most of the buddies, friends, and teammates dropped out of the baseball picture.) It wasn't all fun and games. I often wondered when their enthusiasm would flag. There were many other activities they had to miss and lots of cold meals waiting for them at home. But they kept insisting on working hard to improve their strengths and compensate for their weaknesses. They've all had to overcome injuries, discouragement, uncooperative college schedules, or various coaches' idiosyncrasies in order to keep playing the game; but the results have been astonishing.

This summer a scout from the Tampa Bay Devil Rays showed up on our front doorstep and signed Matthew to a professional contract as a power-hitting outfielder. A few days later we received a call from the Anaheim Angels who needed a left-handed pitcher in their bull pen.

Who knows how much longer each of them will choose to stay in the game! But what started as a $2.99 toy turned into a life-changing investment.

As parents, we got them started and taught them a little about baseball along the way. But our kids have taught us major lessons about determination, perseverance, and enjoyment of the gifts God has given them. They have each invested a lot of time and energy in the sport, but they've also received a lot of compensation for their dedication.

 Baseball has taken them across the country and even to Africa, where Zach participated on a summer Athletes in Action baseball team. They have had many outstanding experiences, received college scholarships, made new friends, and had countless opportunities to share their faith.

And me? I've had the unique privilege of raising an "Angel" and a "Devil"!

My prayer for today:

Thank You, Lord, for the lessons You constantly teach me through my children. Their perseverance and diligence in developing the talents You have given them inspire me. It encourages me to be dedicated and industrious in my role as a parent. It prods me to persist when my tasks seem

overwhelming. Teach me to value hard work more than trite
pleasures; to toil more than I talk. Give me a *persevering*
heart, dear God, one that delights in the talents and sticks to
the tasks You have assigned.

Amen.

ABOUT THE AUTHOR

Gwendolyn Mitchell Diaz's life experiences emerge from a variety of venues and vocations, all of which have added incredible insight and background to her role as a mom. She spent the first nine years of her life in Nigeria, West Africa, as a "missionary kid" growing up in a mud brick house with no electricity or running water. Her years adapting to life in the United States included sports and scholarly pursuits.

A graduate of the University of Pennsylvania, Gwen spent several years working as a school nurse while she honed her writing skills. For five years, she wrote a weekly newspaper column focusing on family issues and incidents. She has also been a feature writer for several national magazines.

Gwen and her husband, Ed, have been married for twenty-eight years. Together they are raising four active sons, a male dog, and a neutered cat. While peering over piles of laundry and gazing around sacks of groceries, Gwen has often been able to find significance and humor in the everyday moments of life as these entertaining anecdotes attest.

Additional copies of this book
are available from your local bookstore.

If you have enjoyed this book or if it has
impacted your life, we would like to hear from you.
Please contact us at:

Honor Books
Department E
P.O. Box 55388
Tulsa, Oklahoma 74155